Toward a
Post-Digital Society

Where Digital Evolution Meets People's Revolution

Antonio Grasso

First published 2023 by DeltalogiX

ISBN 9798865436393

Copyright © Antonio Grasso 2023

The information provided in this book is intended for informational and
educational purposes only. The author has made every effort to ensure the
accuracy and completeness of the information contained herein. However,
the author and the publisher are not responsible for any errors, omissions,
or for the results obtained from the use of this information. The opinions
expressed in this book are solely those of the author.

For permission requests, write to:
DeltalogiX Srl
Viale Degli Astronauti 8
80131 - Napoli - Italy

To my mother, who remains my guiding star even though she is no longer with us. Her love and wisdom are forever imprinted on my heart, always showing me the right path. May her memory continue to light my way.

Contents Page

INTRODUCTION
A bridge between two eras

Digitalization has been an ever-present thread running throughout my life and career. I have been at the forefront of digitalization: a software programmer, developer and architect before most people had ever heard those words, let alone knew what those jobs entailed. I helped to build the first wave of digitalization that began to sweep through everyone's lives. Later, I rode at the crest of that wave as a CEO, adviser to multinationals, and thought leader addressing large conference audiences and over a million followers on social media platforms. I've been an enthusiastic early adopter of consumer technology, from the first PC to the smartphone to Alexa and the autonomous car. But now, that era of digitalization has reached a bridge – a crossing to the next era. The entrance to the bridge reads 'To the post-digital future'. It is a one-way bridge; turning back is not an option. We are being pushed across by technological progress, whether we like it or not. I happen to like it and will explain over the course of this book why we should all embrace this positive new reality. However, there are potential dangers that we must prepare for along the way. The Post-Digital Society will envelop us all, with huge implications for business, lifestyle, the environment, and leisure. And the window of time that we have to prepare and adapt is very short. This book will prepare you, and hopefully enthuse you, for an active role in the Post-Digital Society.

*

I fell in love with electronics and computing when I was at the school. I grew up in Naples – the beautiful city in Southern Italy where I still live. But studying at that time meant attending the Technical Institute. With two older sisters who were already studying, my family could not afford to send me to university too. While I attended the Technical Institute, I learned about computer hardware, transistors, and ports, but I wasn't learning anything about the software. So, I did something interesting. I walked up to the University of Naples and knocked on the door of the Professor of Computing and Electrical Engineering. I explained my situation and I asked which books I should buy to study the course by myself, in my own time. He gave me the full program, while one of my uncle's loaned me the money to buy the books. The first three books, which I still remember, were: *Programming in COBOL*. COBOL was my first coding language one of the first commercial languages used. *Database Administration*, which covered the basics. And the third was unexpected: *An Introduction to Microeconomics*. I remember saying to the professor, "sorry, but I want to program computers?!". He said "Yes, Antonio, you need the first book to understand the programming language, the other to cover databases, but if you want to study computer engineering you need to also understand microeconomics'. That was a foundational moment for me. I understood from the very start that the processes of business, and the processes of computing, are intrinsically linked.

I don't know why I fell so in love with software and computing, but love isn't always rational. When you fall in love with a woman, you don't always know why. The same was happening to me at that time. It was something burning inside me. I started reading those books every night, sometimes all through the night. Then I was excited to discover that in my apartment building was a start-up an IT company. And they had a computer. Nobody had personal computers in 1983 – the computer was only for companies and wealthy individuals. I asked them if I could practice with theirs. I was only 18-19. I said I'd work for them without pay, I didn't care, I just wanted to practice, to feel the touch of the keyboard. They said "okay, Antonio, come in the afternoon from 4pm to 6pm, we have a workstation you can use". That was the start of everything. There was no stopping me. I had a natural gift for programming. They couldn't believe what I was capable of. I remember them saying, astonished, "How are you programming software without being trained?" What could I say: when you feel passion, everything is natural. They soon hired me on full pay, saying "Antonio, you're a genius!" I don't think I was or am, by the way, but so few people had the skills in those days that I was a revelation to them. I started with that company writing software, without any limitation, with the computer at my fingertips. It was an open book, to me. I wrote software from 1983 to 2003.

That small company was a partner of the big tech company NCR. At that time NCR was a fierce competitor of IBM. I started on a Minicomputer for general purpose administrative business use, writing in COBOL. I then moved on to the personal computer (PC) with MS DOS, the first disk operating system and the precursor to Windows. And then came the Unix, open architecture environment.

When I left that company I moved to the retail sector and then to the industrial sector. In previous decades, switching from one sector to another would not have been an easy task – many people entered one workforce straight from school, and only left when they retired. I didn't know it then, but I was amongst the first wave of IT professionals to benefit from the fluidity of digitalization. The ability to move seamlessly between sectors in the 'gig economy' is normal now, but in the 80s it was only just becoming available to those of us who worked directly with computers. When I switched to the industrial sector, I felt no change – because when you program, when you develop software, the language remains exactly the same.

In 1993, I walked into IBM's headquarters in Naples, carrying a couple of CD-ROMs. I wanted to use the RISC System/6000, the company's first Unix machine, to test the source code of my own business management application, which was written in COBOL. Although the machine was conceived of as a workstation for graphics applications with the X Window system (X11), I had been tasked with porting our software to assess its applications and suitability for business environments. On my first attempt, I was unable to complete the process because a third-party component had to be adapted to the new environment. But once everything was in place, I ran some source compiling and was amazed by how fast the RISC/6000 system could crunch through the code. Immediately, I understood that this would change everything.

I was then a partner in a business management software development company that operated in a vertical sector: industrial engineering, production planning, and control. We were already specialists and had our share of successes, but were only able to do our real market launch thanks to our partnership with IBM. The big IT companies were creating an ecosystem in which we all could flourish.

When I made that first porting, I was the first software developer to port a management application on the RISC/6000 not just in Naples, but in the whole of Italy. IBM gave me generous benefits and made me an IBM Business Partner. That was the first big shift in my career. During that partnership I developed completely new software for construction and engineering companies to manage their resources, materials, and project timelines. In no time we soon captured 20% of the market. IBM made my software available on all IBM computers.

Next I joined a company that worked with the public sector – again, another previously unimaginable, but now seamless, switch – specifically government Ministries. This was the early 2000s, and a big moment for digital transformation in government processes. It was really an interesting time. I became a software architect at a high level with a team of software developers working under me, but I never stopped designing software. Every time I talk with a customer, even now, the software builds in my mind. But for the first time I had a team to also write code for me. I worked with the Ministry of Interior in Italy. Immigration was becoming a big public issue, so the department received a lot of funds to digitize the immigration process, including visa requests and citizenship. Government processes began to look similar to business processes, with government organizations that worked and looked like a company. I built the first workflow management system software, and we began to connect it up with other ministries. For the first time, the Minister of Interior was connected with other ministries and Ministers via a single digital platform. It was around this time that the words 'digital transformation' and 'digitalization' became widely used. There was a clear change and shift from one world to another: from paper-based bureaucracy (using that word in its purest form) to something digitized and easily accessible.

After that, I started a new experience in the US with the

financial sector. I was fascinated by the financial sector – NASDAQ, trading, this was all new and exciting to me, especially coming out of my work in the public sector. I am still tied to a nondisclosure agreement with them, so I cannot disclose their name, but they're one of the biggest investment companies in the world. They were trying to build the first ever software for an automated trading mechanism and were searching the world for an innovative software developer capable of seeing it through. They approached me, and I said yes, but only if I can stay in Naples. I love Naples, I love the sea, I love my city. So, they said ok, "it's a deal!". Again, I was ahead of the curve, working remotely, online-only with another country – it is common now, but it was unheard of then. It was an amazing experience, and the five-year contract soon became six. I was developing one of the first robotic approaches for trading exchanges. I made the money that allowed me to start my own company, Digital Business Innovation, in 2016.

I wanted to give that briefest of overview of my career to show you how digitalization was building like a wave that propelled me and society forwards, concurrently. The old processes of the past were being shed one-by-one, and I was on the front line. I was a digital warrior. In the next chapter we will look at how the embryonic Post-Digital Society began to form because of this. But first, let's take a little time to talk about the era of digitalization that we're still living in, and how it happened. I remember some of the claims in the 1990s and early 2000s about what a digital world might be like. But when it arrived, the reality was even more dramatic than people expected.

*

The digital era began with Alan Turing and the 'universal Turing machine' during the second world war. But from then until arguably the early 1980s, computers and computing remain a closed shop. Computers were not only the size of whole rooms, but they were also closely guarded behind lock and key. It was only freed from these confines thanks to the microchip. ENIAC, the US Army's computer in 1946 which built upon Turing's design, originally used 18,000 vacuum tubes to calculate artillery trajectories more quickly and accurately than any human. But it was huge and unreliable – when a single tube failed (which it did on average, every two days) the entire machine would shut down. William Shockley, a London-born American physicist, improved the vacuum tube by discovering that certain chemical elements could perform a similar function of encoding and transmitting 1s and 0s. Shockley developed the theory of semiconduction and set his colleagues John Bardeen and Walter Brattain to work on a practical device to manipulate electrical current on a semiconductor, leading to the first working transistor. Despite Shockley's Nobel Prize in physics in 1956, he was known to be unpleasant and hard to work for, and his company, Shockley Semiconductor, imploded. The full story is told in Chris Miller's recent book 'Chip War: The Fight for the World's Most Critical Technology' (Simon and Schuster, 2022). The "traitorous eight", a group of talented engineers who left Shockley's company, instead founded Fairchild Semiconductor, which became the birthplace of the modern semiconductor industry. One of the eight, Gordon Moore, was the driving force behind the accelerating capacity of microchips – and has 'Moore's Law' (the theory that chips double in power or halve in price every eighteen months) named after him. The moment when Iraq was bombed with a barrage of microchip guided missiles in 1991, Miller writes, "the Cold War was over; Silicon Valley had won."[1]

But that's only the story of how computerization came to benefit big industry and the military. What of the digitalization of everyday life, and the emergence of the digital society? This, in my opinion, began when the personal computer (PC) became commercially available. That was the start of the digital era. Computers broke out of their enclosed environments and data centers, and began to spread throughout the public realm. From 1980 to 1985, the first personal computers for business people became available. The next step was the Laptop and desktop computer for personal use in the 1990s, combined with the Internet. We began to be able to connect with each other, with email and photo attachments, using search engines to ask and answer any question without having to reach for a physical book or Encyclopedia. But it was typically something we could turn off and on. We still might, in between, switch off, pick up a newspaper, walk into town with no expectation of meeting anyone in particular, just whomever you might bump into.

But then in 2010 the smartphone arrived, and the digital era fully took over. The smartphone was the great leap forward for digitalization. There is a direct line from the PC to the laptop/internet, and finally to the smartphone. But of the three, it was only the smartphone, just 12 or 13 years before this very book was written, that was the big leap in democratizing, personalizing, and mobilizing digitalization. Digital became essential. It was no longer something we accessed only at work or college. It became a natural part of our daily lives. There was no 'turning it off'.

It also began something that will become a foundation of the Post-Digital Society: people started creating the content. With the 'user generated content', the role and power of individuals changed. And not just for young early adopters. For everyone. Your Grandmother was soon on Facebook. Previously we had only consumed content generated for us by mainstream media, TV, newspapers, professional journalists, actors, filmmakers. We were passive in receiving that content: watch this movie, listen to this song, read this article, buy this book. But the smartphone realized our desire to *be on the stage*. We didn't have to be *told* anymore – it was us who could do the telling. User generated content via social media saw new professions, new roles emerge: influencers, the creator economy, 'pro-sumers', the gig economy.

The creator economy is a foundational pillar of the Post-Digital Society, which we will analyze in Chapter One. In my opinion, the shift to a Post-Digital Society started when we began generating content by ourselves: making a post on social media, writing a blog article on Medium, sharing our restaurant choices on Instagram, making a short Infotainment film on TikTok. We began to choose our own trajectory. That is: we want to count, we want to be on the stage, we are the democracy. If you watch early YouTube clips, we didn't know how to use it – it was mostly shaky home-videos, like a blooper reel or 'Candid Camera' of everyday life. But now we all have the tools to make professional-quality videos, presentations, graphs, infographics, often just using free online tools. TikTok influencers are producing content that would have required a professional team to produce just 10 years ago; now anyone can do it from their bedroom. This rapid deployment of professional tools to the masses is truly liberating and democratic. Keep that in mind when someone says that "everything is getting worse with technology" – I would say that everything is getting better. There is far more possibility for us to reach our potential now that such tools are no longer exclusive to large organizations or wealthy individuals. This has transformed the business world too, where start-up disruptor companies can enter new markets and overtake, even destroy, centuries-old legacy companies. If you are a CEO of one such legacy company reading this, you may wonder what the good news is. But don't worry – the flipside is that consumers and talented employees are also more accessible than ever.

As digitalization became part of everyone's daily lives, via the smartphone, this brought benefits. But it also shed light on some darker sides of human nature. People on social media 24 hours a day, who go to sleep with the phone in their hand, are displaying pathological behaviors. But that is the exception. Digitalization allowed us all to manifest in new ways without being a sub-product of the mainstream. We have breached the mainstream. Now, there is disintermediation and decentralization from the traditional forms of media. An individual can have a YouTube channel with 50 million subscribers. That's also created an ethical problem, because the creator must respond and be accountable for what they create. As with every step of progress mankind has ever taken, this has created pros and cons. One of the big issues I see is private groups on WhatsApp or Facebook or Twitter/X, which leads to closed groups. Everyone has the same opinion on the same matter. Their concern about something mounts because of the amplification within closed silos; what's become known as the 'echo chamber' effect. Consider Flat Earthers as an example of how people can be convinced of something that is false. How is it possible to convince people that the Earth is flat? We've known since Pythagoras, Aristotle, and Eratosthenes made calculations of the Earth's circumference in the third century BCE, that the earth is spherical. We've known since Galileo that the Sun is the center of the solar system. Now we have astronauts in orbit, we have the ISS, a rover on Mars. It is irrefutable. Yet this is the power of the closed group – and this power should not be underestimated. Because everyone is saying the same thing and reinforcing the other's shared views, we become more and more entrenched. Similarly in the USA, QAnon conspiracies and their ilk have led to polarization. Closed groups in social media have created the polarization now affecting real life society. The Republicans and Democrats are more polarized than ever. We see the same in the UK with Brexit, in Italy with the rise of 'Brothers of Italy'. In fact, in all democratic countries, social media can create polarization – this polarization is fostered and amplified among closed groups, who then emerge in the real world utterly convinced, after months or years of online reinforcement of the same message, that they are right. Picture the QAnon-driven mob that led the January 6 United States Capitol attack. This is one of the big issues we need to fix. But is this the 'fault' of technology or digitalization? I would say not. Closed groups and echo chambers are the issue, not the tools themselves. The Post-Digital Society will, and must, engage more with open, democratic forums, where all voices are heard – we will look at how in Chapter Two. In short, digitalization is accelerating everything: the good and the bad. If we enter the Post-Digital Society with open eyes and open minds, we will have the choice of which of the two paths we want to take.

*

When I founded my business Digital Business Innovation (DBI) in 2016, the traditional method of building the company would have been designing a logo and relentlessly advertising the brand. But understanding the trajectory of digitalization, I decided to do it in a different way. The brand was me. My entrepreneurship, my experience, was the real value of this company. In the start-up world, you and the business are the same entity. This is why I started on social media using my name Antonio Grasso, not Digital Business Innovation. Yes, DBI is a channel, but a small channel. The real capital, the real value, was me, and my knowledge. I started talking about my technological expertise, and became influential on Twitter/X, LinkedIn, Instagram, Facebook and Medium. This was the new approach, entirely in-keeping with the creator-led economy: don't put the company on stage, put yourself on the stage.

I had ridden that first nascent wave of digitalization – I had been there from the very start. But now I was benefitting from a larger wave that had washed over the whole of society. I have a double role as an entrepreneur, managing project for Italian companies. But my biggest revenue comes from creating content for large multinational companies: articles, video, infographics. They want my expertise because they know that the world is changing from advertising to organic growth. I've recently collaborated with British Telecom, for example, turning their latest research into easily digestible infographics and video. In turn, this establishes me as a global thought leader. I feel uncomfortable being self-aggrandizing, but across my channels I have over 1 million followers globally. I am justifiably known as a global thought leader.

I still design software – and my daughter, Linda, is an engineer in my company now. I made sure she had the chance to study at university. But I still recommended that she read the book on Microeconomics. But in the last two to three years, I began witnessing the shift from digital to the early signs of post-digital, and I realized that it will transform the world again, for the second time in my lifetime.

I already see companies changing, and people changing their behaviors. If I go home and switch on the light, and discover that I have no power, it is a disaster – we are totally dependent on power at home, and we expect it to always be there. Similarly, if you turn on the tap for water and no water comes out, it is a catastrophe – how can we live without water at home? When I was two or three years old living on the rural periphery of Naples, there was no electricity or running water at home in 1965-1966. We had no restroom at all – the restroom was outside. What was normal then is totally alien now, it sounds like centuries ago. The same will happen in a Post-Digital Society. A 24/7 Internet-of-Things (IoT) will be as normal, as expected, as demanded, as water and electricity. Maslow's hierarchy of needs will have to be updated. In fact, Guo Ping, Rotating

CEO at Huawei, recognized exactly this in a speech in Nov 2017, arguing for a new digital hierarchy of needs:

- **Bottom layer:** ICT infrastructure – the foundation of digital economy.

- **Second layer:** security, for both the physical and digital worlds.

- **Third layer:** industrial digitization and Industry 4.0.

- **Top layer:** a digital AI brain to help coordinate management, utilizing Big Data.[2]

DIGITAL TRANSFORMATION
A country's hierarchy of needs

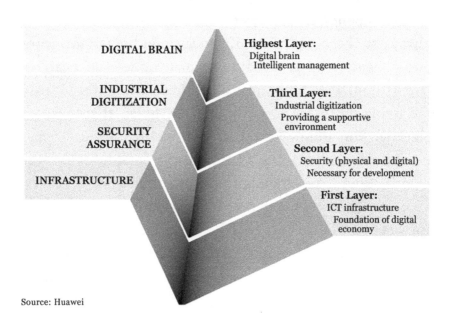

DIGITAL BRAIN

INDUSTRIAL DIGITIZATION

SECURITY ASSURANCE

INFRASTRUCTURE

Highest Layer:
Digital brain
Intelligent management

Third Layer:
Industrial digitization
Providing a supportive environment

Second Layer:
Security (physical and digital)
Necessary for development

First Layer:
ICT infrastructure
Foundation of digital economy

Source: Huawei

We will soon not notice digital anymore because it will be intricately woven into everything we do. We can already see this in Digital Natives – those born from 2010 onwards. They don't care about or even know what 'digital' is – it's just normal life. They have seen the smartphone from birth. For Millennials, Gen X, Baby Boomers, it was something new. But for Gen Z, if you ask them – and try asking this yourself as an experiment, when you talk to people who are 12-14 years old – "How does it feel being born with digital and using digital every day?" They will likely respond "What is 'digital'? I don't use digital". This is the switch happening right now: when we do not notice digital because it's an integral part of life. *That* is the starting point of the Post-Digital Society.

As a child I played with toy metal cars. I knew it was a toy – only my imagination could make it something more than that. Now, if I need to play with a car, I play X Box, a hyper-realistic digital representation of car racing. People born in 2020 won't differentiate between the physical and digital in the same way, because they look the same. In recent times we have even seen News bulletins mistakenly including scenes from video games, tricking even Picture Editors into thinking they were real images from war zones. Soon, we will meet up with friends and business partners in the Metaverse – our avatars will become part of who we are and how we live. This is life already for 14-year-old gamers. In the next 10-15 years, it will be all our lives.

Running parallel to this same seismic shift, is climate change. What does the Post-Digital Society have to say, what does it have to offer, for a world of increased temperatures, extreme weather, and an urgent need to drive carbon emissions down to Net Zero? The Paris Agreement requires us to be climate-neutral –economies with net-zero greenhouse gas emissions – by 2050[3]. Precisely the same timeframe that I envision the Post-Digital Society taking over. I will address these questions throughout the book, and in detail in Chapter Six.

When I became a father, I felt a lot of responsibility for my daughter's future. The science convinced me that yes, climate change is something that is organic to the Earth, but not in this short time frame. Climate science shows us that the global temperature can change by one degree in 2000 years, that the Earth is used to manage this kind of changing climate – but not one degree in 30 years! That is unbelievable. And so, I felt the need to take action. I'm not one to go on the street protesting. But rather I realized that the business world I was working in, consulting and advising, was at the forefront of the fight against climate change, offering great hope for the Post-Digital Society. Cryptocurrency and blockchain will be integral to the Post-Digital Society, but it has gotten off to a shaky start. Bitcoin, the early front-runner, is consuming a lot of energy, because the blockchain needs to be recalculated from the start, each time: all the transactions from the first Bitcoin to the last. This technology is called DLT, distributed ledger technology, and there are already alternatives to blockchain, like Tangle. The problem is that the success of the Bitcoin was unregulated, the first experiment. But now everyone is aware of the blockchain 'mining' problem, and everyone now is collaborating within the community to fix the issue. We will go into this more deeply later in the book, but in short, the solution is creating a tamper proof stop, so you don't need to recalculate everything from the beginning. Cryptocurrency's problems will soon be solved, and become the foundation of a low-emissions, decentralized society.

Many people also misjudge the power of the Internet-of-Things (IoT) and simply a fridge or dishwasher that sends you a friendly message to say 'I'm done!'. But a fridge telling you that the milk has gone off is just basic marketing. In the Post-Digital Society, the autonomous vehicle is IoT, able to recharge itself with off-peak, renewable energy, and save lives because of fewer crashes. Or the medical device on your wrist that can send information automatically to the doctor in real time. At the moment it is new and amusing to ask Alexa to turn off the lights. That's because we are still approaching post-digital; we still make a distinction between the physical and the digital. But soon there will be no such boundary. It'll just be there. In the Post-Digital Society, I will ask Alexa 'I need to go home now – please send me a car'. And then an autonomous car will come. You don't need to learn to drive. You *can* go to the pub and 'drive' home. In an electric autonomous car, you can even sleep while the car is driving you home. *That* is the transformative change we need to focus on.

This is an important historical moment, and one that will never come again. We are preparing to cross the bridge between the digital and post-digital eras. We are witnessing the relentless, unstoppable advance of technology. Day by day, we become aware of a new technology that is enabling things that we did not imagine before. We cannot have imagined some years ago or even some months ago something like Chat GPT responding in a way that looks like a human. Given my experience from the dawn of digitalization to its realization, now is the perfect moment for me to write a book which considers what the post-digital future will be like. What was once a futuristic vision has become a reality. This book will help you to understand the changes happening in our daily life, in our work, in our businesses, and in our politics. The younger generation are already there. They live in a post-digital life. We are at the breakthrough stage – after that comes acceleration. Only now do we have the opportunity to step back, understand the implications, and prepare accordingly. Because all our lives are about to change.

CHAPTER ONE

The five foundations of the Post-Digital Society

In November 2016, The World Economic Forum (WEF) released a seemingly innocuous video outlining '8 predictions for the world in 2030'. The first prediction was "You'll own nothing. And you'll be happy". The reaction to this message, often misattributed to Klaus Schwab (but which came in fact from his WEF colleague, Danish politician Ida Auken), was almost uniformly negative. Horrified responses on WEF's Facebook page included, "George Washington claimed that individual property ownership is the foundation for individual freedoms. I will never give it up."[4] Influential bloggers such as Isaiah McCall have rephrased it "8 Deadly Predictions", describing the WEF as "a Dr. Evil-esque Orwellian organization" and the idea of zero ownership as "terrifying"[5]. The British right-wing publication *The Spectator* asked, "Is Klaus Schwab the greatest threat of our time?"[6] But WEF, Schwab and Auken were right. And they were right about us – eventually – being happy about it, too.

A year after the WEF predictions, in November 2017, Auken wrote a longer article for Forbes explaining the concept further. She wrote the following from the perspective of a citizen in 2030:

"I don't own anything. I don't own a car. I don't own a house. I don't own any appliances or any clothes... Everything you considered a product, has now become a service. We have access to transportation, accommodation, food and all the things we need in our daily lives. One by one all these things became free, so it ended up not making sense for us to own much."[7]

WEF and Auken weren't describing a terrifying *removal* of goods and wealth at all – they were merely describing servitization, decentralization and disintermediation. In 2016 when WEF first made the prediction, Spotify and Netflix had just 40 million and 70 million subscribers worldwide. By Q4 of 2022, they had 205 million and 230 million globally[8]. Once cherished CD and DVD collections, and their sales, have all but disappeared; thousands of pounds of assets and many meters of shelf-space were freed up, replaced by apps costing just €5-10 a month. The trend is clear, and it is set to become the norm for the Post-Digital Society. We'll own nothing (or very little). And we'll be happier, healthier, and in more control, because of it. In this chapter we will look at the forces that led to Auken's imagined citizen in 2030. I call these The Five Foundations of the Post-Digital Society.

Foundation 1: Personalization and Servitization

The trend that Auken described has become known as 'Servitization'. This is our first 'Foundation' of the Post-Digital Society. And we are perhaps already halfway through our transition towards a full Servitization Economy.

With the shift from industry to services, information technologies, and automation, we formed a new economic model. Looking back, it's hard to imagine that anyone could have predicted this development during the industrial age. With servitization, the post-digital era is poised to bring about unprecedented changes to global society and the economy.

Kevin Kelly, the founding editor of *Wired* magazine, in his book "The Inevitable: Understanding the 12 Technological Forces That Will Shape Our Future," suggests – as do I – that technology is becoming so ubiquitous and integrated into our lives that we will no longer notice it as something separate. Or, as he puts it, "This is not a race against the machines. This is a race *with* the machines."[9] Echoing WEF, he writes, "Possession is not as important as it once was. Accessing is more important than ever." The true ‹post-digital› age is when we›re no longer aware of 'digital' as something separate. We don't see it as a distinct phenomenon, but rather as the very stuff of life.

Amy Webb, futurist and founder of the Future Today Institute, also believes that the Post-Digital Society centers around technology becoming more personalized and individualized. She suggests that as technology becomes more sophisticated, it will be able to anticipate our needs and desires and will tailor its offerings to suit our individual preferences. In her book "The Signals Are Talking: Why Today's Fringe Is Tomorrow's Mainstream," Webb writes:

> "In 1990s, we had transitioned away from the era of personal computing to a fourth era the internet, which was democratizing how information was shared. Everyday people were getting online to help build this new frontier... This fourth era is nothing at all like what those earlier computing experts had predicted. Everyday people, not just programmers, are able to configure smartphones to their liking, adding and removing apps as they design their own".[i]

As I stated in the Introduction, the commercial arrival of the PC marked the beginning of the digital era. For the first time, computing was no longer confined to data centers staffed by clinical, white-coated technicians. The simple fact that it was now accessible to the general public marked an enormous shift and paved the way for the digital revolution (or 'fourth era', in Webb's terminology) that

---

[i] Webb, Amy. The Signals Are Talking: Why Today's Fringe Is Tomorrow's Mainstream. PublicAffairs, 2016.

would soon follow. However, the true democratization of computational power didn't occur until the late 2000s, when the smartphone burst onto the scene. Suddenly, the digital world was at our fingertips, available to us no matter where we were or the time of day. This remarkable shift in accessibility changed the way we interacted with technology and with each other in ways that we are only beginning to fully understand. The smartphone profoundly impacted our behavior and sense of place. But its most significant impact was to generate a newfound awareness of the role of the individual within social and economic systems. The dawn of digitalization gave us a stronger sense of control and freedom over our actions, irrespective of geographical or social constraints.

This personalization paved the way for us to play a more direct and autonomous role in shaping the dynamics of society, politics, and the economy. The next obvious step was servitization.

Netflix is perhaps the prime example of servitization: it allows you to watch movies without buying or borrowing a DVD or Blu-ray. Instead, you pay a monthly fee to Netflix; Spotify has done the same for music. An interesting example of the servitization still to come, and how it will shape the Post-Digital Society, is the autonomous car. Already my car, an Alfa Romeo Giulia, is at autonomous car level 2: it can brake, accelerate, steer the wheel, all autonomously. In the next 10 to 15 years, we can expect fully autonomous driving to become mainstream, which will disrupt traditional car ownership. You won't need to buy a car, but instead, you'll use an app to call an autonomous car whenever you need one. Currently, big companies like Netflix and Spotify are making big money through Servitization; next, it will be autonomous cars becoming the new normal. This shift will disrupt a lot of people, including professional drivers and truck drivers for delivery. The business model for servitization is different from traditional models, as you don't need a point of sale. Instead, you need a powerful technological platform that can serve millions of people. In the case of car manufacturers, they will have to change their business model because people won't buy cars anymore; instead, only the companies that rent out the autonomous cars will buy them.

Another example is 3D printing, which is already changing industrial manufacturing: you can design and create whatever you need at home without the need for a manufacturing company. Many companies now offer 3D printing services, which allows individuals or businesses to create three-dimensional objects by printing layers of material on top of each other, based on a digital design. Instead of having to outsource the manufacturing process to a third-party supplier, businesses or individuals can now create their own products using 3D printing technology. This has enabled new business models based on servitization. Rather than selling the physical products themselves, businesses can offer 3D printing services to customers.

Customers can provide a digital design for the product they want, and the business can then use 3D printing technology to create the product and deliver it to the customer. This allows customers to obtain the products they want without having to invest in the necessary manufacturing equipment or expertise. Customers can tailor the design to meet their specific needs or preferences, and businesses can create the customized product.

Technology therefore enables new business models, shaped by the paradigm of servitization. This is a big shift that will have a significant impact on traditional business models. John Gerzema, and Michael D'Antonio argued in their 2010 book 'Spend Shift: How the Post-Crisis Values Revolution Is Changing the Way We Buy, Sell, and Live': "As the customer interest shifts from consumption to creation... often there is not an immediate purchase happening." An early example even then was Hulu, with the authors commenting on "Hulu's ability to deliver an entire series, some many years old, to anyone's computer screen. Beyond determining what they want to watch and when, Hulu users also get the chance to review and comment on programs, take clips to post on their own websites, and share as much or as little video as they want with their friends. In essence, the service lets every individual build a personal network, making judgments about thousands of offerings and then announcing those choices to the world." Hulu's then chief of technology, Eric Feng, explained: "That type of experience didn't even exist a few years ago, but because of digital distribution, we are now giving consumers unprecedented amounts of control over their content experience and their content choices."[10] In short: their customers own nothing, and they are happy.

Foundation 2: User Generated Content and the Prosumer

It is my contention, however, that this shift began even before servitization, and before anyone had heard of Spotify or Netflix. It began, in fact, with 'User Generated Content (UGC)' – our next Foundation of the Post-Digital Society. We became the publisher, not just the reader. Facebook and Medium do not create any content. *We* are the content. This was the spark that ignited the Post-Digital Society.

Web 1.0 was characterized by static websites that were created by one person for the use of many; early versions of Yahoo, GeoCities, and AOL, all featured limited interactive elements and little, if any, user-generated content. With the advent of Web 2.0, we became "prosumers" of digital content: the "producer" and "consumer" combined. Prosumers are individuals who not only consume products and services but also actively participate in their production, through the use of digital technologies. This blurring of the line between producer and consumer is a key feature of the Post-Digital Society. Alvin Toffler, futurist and author of the 1980 book 'The Third Wave', was one of the first thinkers to describe the emergence of the prosumer (and indeed coined the term). In his prescient book, Toffler argued that as digital technologies become more ubiquitous, individuals will become more empowered to produce their own content and participate in the creation of new products and services. Incredibly, given that most people – including me – hadn't even touched a Personal Computer at the time he was writing, and the internet wasn't yet invented, he already recognized that: "Prosumers represent a new stage in the evolution of the economy, one in which consumers become producers and producers become consumers."[11]

The ensuing digital age encouraged us to become more socially engaged, leading us to share a wide range of content, such as videos, photos, texts, articles, and self-published books. As we grew motivated by the interaction and feedback we received from others, companies started sponsoring their products or services on these platforms by paying the owner instead of creating content themselves. With the rise of social media, video sharing and blogging platforms, some sites recognized the potential of content creators and chose to share a portion of their advertising revenue with them. This led to the emergence of individuals known as "influencers" and later "digital creators," who leveraged their online presence to create content and, in some cases, earn a living. With my technological skills and years of experience, I have become one of those creators, sharing my knowledge and experience on social media to create lucrative business opportunities that complement my entrepreneurial IT initiatives.

Such sites only work because of *what we post*. While the site owner takes care of managing the IT infrastructure to ensure that the service runs smoothly, we do the bulk of the work. We do it because there are other peers on the platform with whom we want to collaborate and share our work (or simply for trivial exhibitionism, it doesn't matter!). The essential thing to understand is the shift in our role from simple consumers of digital content to producers of the same. Expressing ourselves, being heard, being on stage for the first time, gave us freedom and control; and once we experienced it, it began to pervade every aspect of society. We no longer wanted to be told and dictated to, we wanted to be heard, and that changed our relationship with the establishment and businesses forever. The days of the consumer were at an end; the dawn of the 'prosumer' began to rise above the horizon.

More recently (but still pre-dating the Smartphone) Yochai Benkler, a scholar of law and technology at Harvard University, argued that the rise of user-generated content is transforming the way we think about production and consumption. In his 2006 book 'The Wealth of Networks', Benkler argues:

> "The emergence of the networked information economy has the potential to increase individual autonomy. First, it increases the range

and diversity of things that individuals can do for and by themselves. It does this by lifting, for one important domain of life, some of the central material constraints... typified the industrial information economy. The majority of materials, tools, and platforms necessary for effective action in the information environment are in the hands of most individuals... This decreases the extent to which individuals are subject to being acted upon by the owners of the facilities on which they depend for communications. The construction of consumers as passive objects of manipulation that typified television culture has not disappeared overnight, but it is losing its dominance in the information environment... It does so by enabling sources commercial and noncommercial, mainstream and fringe, domestic or foreign, to produce information and communicate with anyone. This diversity radically changes the universe of options that individuals can consider as open for them to pursue."[12]

What Benkler refers to as 'the networked information economy' is transforming the way we think about the relationship between production and consumption, blurring the line between producers and consumers. The emergence of prosumers and user-generated content ushered in a fundamental shift in the way we create and consume goods and services. As technology becomes more ubiquitous and more individuals are able to participate in the production of content, the traditional boundaries between producer and consumer became increasingly blurred. This will also be a key aspect of the shift toward a more participatory, collaborative, and democratic society.

Foundation 3: The Creator Economy

The creator economy is the twin sister of user generated content. But it is the capitalist twin. It refers to the growing ecosystem of individuals who use digital platforms to monetize their creativity and expertise across multiple platforms. Once user generated content became the norm, we realized the need to, in a capitalist society, make money from it. We could no longer give our work away for free. A wide range of content creators, such as YouTubers, bloggers, podcasters, and social media influencers had built large followings by producing content that resonates with their audiences and by leveraging the power of social media to promote their work. Now they needed payment.

While user generated content refers to any content created and uploaded by users, the creator economy encompasses a more sophisticated business model. In the creator economy, individuals can build and monetize their brand and creative content, which can range from videos, music, writing, podcasts, to social media posts, and other digital products. The creator economy is about individuals building their own businesses around their content, rather than simply contributing content to existing platforms. In the creator economy, creators often have a dedicated audience, which they engage with and create content for regularly. As I explained in the Introduction, to my surprise, after a long career in software development, I found myself joining the creator economy post 2016 as an influencer, thought-leader, and content creator. The audience is loyal and invested in the creator's brand – like mine – which creates an opportunity for the creator to monetize their content through various channels such as brand sponsorships, merchandise sales, or subscriptions. Again, in contrast, user generated content is often created and uploaded to platforms such as social media with no expectation of monetary compensation.

This shift resulted in the democratization of the creative process, empowering individuals to build and monetize their own brands, rather than having to rely on established, legacy media organizations. This new business model is fueled by the democratization of the creative process and empowered by digital technologies that made it easier for individuals to create and distribute their content online. As Li Jin, co-founder of Variant Fund and a Harvard Business Review author, writes, "Creator platforms flourish when they provide opportunity for anyone to grow and succeed... creators are the new small businesses." She continues that the creator economy (she also uses the term 'passion economy'): "is rooted in and celebrates the notion of creator leverage: Because creators emphasize their individuality and offer unique services/products that are non-fungible, creators wield much more power over platforms than gig workers who are entirely replaceable."[13]

In the Post-Digital Society, the creator economy is likely to become ever more central to society as people increasingly turn from mainstream media to decentralized platforms for their entertainment, social connection, and even education. As traditional jobs become less stable and reliable, more people are likely to turn to content creation as a means to generate income and build a personal brand. This can be seen in a positive light, as Gary Drenik, CEO of Prosper Business Development, wrote in Forbes in 2022: "With 50 million people identifying themselves as 'creators', marketers are investing more of their social media budgets in content creator partnerships to take hold of this growing opportunity. This momentum is only expected to continue, putting the creator economy on a path to further grow and thrive."[14] He found that the majority of marketers (74%) planned to invest at least a quarter of their social media budgets on content creator partnerships in Q4 2022 and Q1 2023.

The rise of NFTs (non-fungible tokens) is also likely to play a significant role in the creator economy as a digital asset that represents ownership of a unique piece of content, such as a digital artwork, video clip, or tweet. By allowing creators to sell their work directly to fans and collectors, NFTs could enable a new era of digital entrepreneurship and empower creators to take control of their own financial destinies. The creator economy, then, will be a key driver of innovation and growth in the post-digital era, as individuals 'leverage' their creativity and expertise to build new businesses and forge new connections with audiences around the world.

While NFTs have gained a lot of attention and notoriety in recent years, particularly from the art world, there are concerns that the current NFT market is speculative and overhyped. While this may be true in their current guise, their emergence also suggests that there is a demand for unique digital assets and that NFTs could be a way to authenticate and monetize them. Handled correctly, NFTs can play an important role in the creator economy and the sharing economy by providing a new way for creators to monetize their digital content and retain ownership over their intellectual property. By creating and selling unique digital assets, creators can use NFTs to verify ownership, establish authenticity, and receive payment for their work. As Dr. Anne-Marie Imafidon, the founder of the social enterprise Stemettes, notes, "NFTs offer a new and exciting way for creators and artists to own and control their digital creations... NFTs can create a transparent and decentralized marketplace for digital content that empowers creators and consumers alike."[15]

By providing individuals with the opportunity to use their skills and talents to create content and earn a living, the creator economy has the potential to democratize the workforce and break down traditional barriers to success. Industry 5.0 will, then, be shaped around personalization. And personalization leads to disintermediation and decentralization.

Foundation 4: Disintermediation and Decentralization

The central foundation of the post digital era (and indeed of this book) is disintermediation and decentralization. Understanding what these represent is essential for anyone seeking to navigate the rapidly changing landscape of the post-digital era. These phenomena have far-reaching implications for all aspects of society, including the very paradigms of peaceful order or conflict.

Disintermediation, the removal of intermediaries in a supply chain or transaction, is a trend borne of the digital era. Online marketplaces such as Amazon or eBay allowed manufacturers to sell directly to consumers, bypassing traditional retail channels. Crowdfunding platforms such as Kickstarter and Indiegogo allowed entrepreneurs to raise money directly from consumers and investors, bypassing traditional sources of funding such as banks and venture capitalists. Ride-sharing services such as Uber and Lyft connected drivers directly with passengers, bypassing traditional taxi companies. All of these met our growing desire to take control, and this quiet, ongoing revolution is cutting out intermediaries in everything from news to finance to (eventually, as we'll see in Chapter Two) political leadership. Not only did individuals begin seeking alternative sources for information, beyond mainstream media, this fueled their urge to play a more direct and autonomous role in purchasing power and democracy.

The rise of cryptocurrency, for example, has shown us that it's possible to create and use currency without the need for central banks to act as intermediaries and gate keepers. There is no longer a need for a central authority, such as a central bank, to create the financial auditing and currency strategy. In Europe, we have the European Central Bank, in the US it's the Fed, and in the UK, the UK Central Bank: each act as intermediaries between consumers and traders who use the money and the government that creates it. However, sometimes major flaws in the system arise. In the USA, for instance, the dollar serves as the world's reserve currency and is essential to the price of oil, referred to as the 'petrodollar'. It is the responsibility of the USA's leaders to maintain a stable dollar, but this has not been the case, as seen in the crash of 2008 and again in early 2023 when the Fed printed billions of dollars to cover debts owed by Silicon Valley Bank. This printing of money poses a risk to us all as it can lead to inflation: someone will have to pay for it, and ultimately that someone is us in the form of taxes. In the case of America, the burden will be global, and the EU is also affected. This problem needs to be fixed, and the US cannot solve it alone.

Blockchain technology could potentially replace the currently flawed financial system, allowing instead for peer-to-peer transactions without the need for intermediaries like central banks. Cryptocurrencies such as Bitcoin and Ethereum operate on decentralized networks that are not controlled by any central authority or government. Decentralized finance (DeFi), also built on blockchain technology, allows for financial transactions to occur without intermediaries such as banks, brokers, or exchanges. Instead, DeFi relies on smart contracts (note: we'll look at smart contracts in more detail later) that automate the execution of financial transactions. Another example is the use of stablecoins, maintained by algorithms and market forces rather than the actions of a central bank. Stablecoins are typically designed to maintain their peg to the underlying asset through various mechanisms, such as the use of smart contracts and algorithms that adjust the supply based on market demand. It is, in a sense, an automated central bank – and in another sense, it entirely replaces the need for central banks.

Decentralization is the driving force behind disintermediation. It seeks to distribute power and functions previously managed centrally to broader levels of stakeholders. More than a fascinating thought experiment, decentralization is a lever that, when pulled, could give way to unprecedented changes for our social and economic order.

To date, social media platforms such as Facebook and Twitter (especially under Musk's ownership) have been highly centralized. But decentralized social media platforms will emerge. We already have one real life example in Mastodon. As I write, we don't yet know if Mastodon itself will flourish, or wither on the vine. But if not Mastodon itself, then something similar will emerge to take its place. Because Mastodon meets the definition of a decentralized social media platform: it is not owned or controlled by a single central entity, such as a corporation or government. Instead, it is run by a network of independently owned and operated servers, known as 'instances', that communicate with each other through a common protocol. Each 'instance' of Mastodon is owned and operated by its own administrator, who has complete control over the policies and rules of the instance. This means that each instance can have its own code of conduct, moderation policies, and user base, while still being part of the wider Mastodon network. Users of Mastodon can choose to create an account on any instance they wish and communicate with users on any other instance within the network. This creates a decentralized, federated system that gives users greater autonomy and control. It is also a system with big potential for innovative businesses and government organizations. For example, Mastodon's federated, decentralized system could be applied in businesses or governments to give people more control over the products and services they use, and to encourage more participatory, community-driven decision-making, while offering ever-more tailored, personalized solutions. In addition – and with my programming mindset in play – Mastodon uses open-source software, which allows anyone to view and modify the underlying code. This gives greater transparency and community involvement in the development of the platform and could again be applied in business or government to encourage more collaborative, community-driven innovation and development.

As I write, looking out at the bridge between the digital age and the Post-Digital Society, these trends towards decentralization and disintermediation seem as clear as day. Yet the current business leaders are anything but decentralized. The post dot.com boom giants such as Facebook, Amazon, and Google, have simply given us larger intermediaries; traditional monopolies that have devoured and dominated the market. However, I believe the move towards decentralization and disintermediation will be unstoppable and will eventually make it unviable for the centralized monopoly giants to maintain their dominance. One of the key advantages of centralized monopoly businesses is their ability to leverage their market power to gain favorable terms from suppliers and therefore offer lower prices to consumers. However, as decentralized platforms and peer-to-peer networks become more widespread, they will provide alternatives that allow suppliers to reach consumers directly, without the need for intermediaries like Amazon, and therefore able to offer even lower prices, undercutting (and cutting out) the middleman.

Decentralized e-commerce platforms that use blockchain technology will allow suppliers to list their products directly and connect with buyers without going through a centralized marketplace. This in turn reduces the fees and commissions that suppliers have to pay to intermediaries and allow them to offer lower prices to consumers while still maintaining a healthy profit margin.

Similarly, decentralized platforms for content creation and distribution could enable creators to connect with their audiences directly, without having to rely on centralized platforms like Amazon-owned Twitch or YouTube. This could give creators more control over their content and allow them to earn a greater share of the revenue generated from their work. Centralized monopoly businesses like Amazon are likely to continue to have significant advantages for some time to come – such businesses have already shown an ability to adapt and evolve in response to changing market conditions. But decentralization and disintermediation are coming, and will disrupt and transform the market, whether they like it or not.

Foundation 5: Blockchain and Smart Contracts

Blockchain, as we've already seen, is a foundation of the post-digital era, providing a secure, decentralized, and transparent system for managing and sharing data. One of the key features of blockchain – as we all know by now – is that it creates an immutable ledger of transactions that cannot be altered, making it a reliable way to track and verify information. In the Post-Digital Society, blockchain will be used to secure and manage various types of digital assets, including financial transactions, digital identity, intellectual property, and even voting records. By using blockchain to store and share this data, it will become much more difficult for hackers or malicious actors to manipulate or steal sensitive information. "Blockchain is more than a technology", as Eva Kaili, Chair of the European Parliament's science and technology panel, has pronounced, "it is an infrastructure upon which we can build wider applications such as the Internet of Things, smart cities and infrastructures"[16]. Kaili has argued that the EU should create a 'passport' for blockchain products, similar to the one created for the trade in financial products, so as to "avoid regulatory fragmentation between EU member states."[17]

Blockchain will create a new paradigm for managing information in the post-digital age. The information it stores is protected by cryptography — i.e., a unique string of numbers that link various blocks and that is virtually impossible to crack. In this way, transactions can be fully controlled without intermediaries. As Don Tapscott, the author of 'Blockchain Revolution', explains in his book:

> "...the blockchain is a distributed ledger representing a network consensus of every transaction that has ever occurred. Like the World

Wide Web of information, it's the World Wide
Ledger of value—a distributed ledger that
everyone can download and run on their personal computer... blockchain technology could be
an important tool for protecting and preserving
humanity and the rights of every human being,
a means of communicating the truth..."[18]

Stripping away the hype around blockchain, we can simply say that it is 'just a database'; a secure, decentralized,
and transparent container that links each data with the
previous data using cryptography. So, each transaction
is linked to the previous transaction via the hash algorithms that reduce the amount of data contained in the
transaction to a single and fixed length string. This string
is then added to the next transaction and recalculated creating the 'chain'.

The power and future role of blockchain, however, cannot
be understood without smart contracts. The smart contract is the real game changer. Think of smart contracts
as the business process enablers for blockchain. Although they function like paper contracts, smart contracts are
agreements between counterparts that are self-executed,
pre-programmed, and written into lines of code. Instead
of relying on a platform with an intermediary, you have
a smart code that introduces us to a concept called 'code
is law'. This refers to predefined rules that are embedded
in the software and cannot be changed if the software is

decentralized and public. To make changes, you need the consensus of 50% plus one of the users of the smart contract. This creates true disintermediation, and it could produce platforms that look like an Etsy, Amazon, or Last-minute.com but are in fact big smart contracts without a company behind it. Although this may seem unimaginable today, I believe it will become a reality, and the code *will* become the law via smart contracts in the Post-Digital Society. No company, only an algorithm: that is the concept of 'code is law'.

SMART CONTRACTS:
Realizing True Benefits of Blockchain

Blockchain is a cryptographic or encoded ledger (database) of
transactions in the form of blocks arranged in a chain

Smart contract, a complex set of software codes with components designed to
automate execution and settlement, is the application layer that makes much of
the benefits of blockchain technology a reality

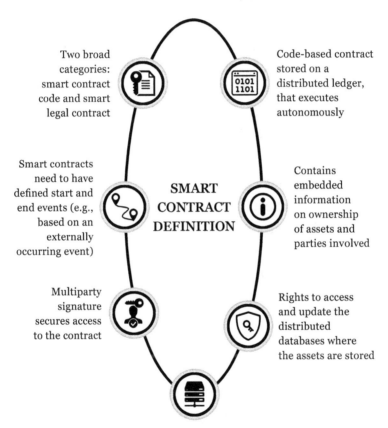

Two broad
categories:
smart contract
code and smart
legal contract

Code-based contract
stored on a
distributed ledger,
that executes
autonomously

Smart contracts
need to have
defined start and
end events (e.g.,
based on an
externally
occurring event)

**SMART
CONTRACT
DEFINITION**

Contains
embedded
information
on ownership
of assets and
parties involved

Multiparty
signature
secures access
to the contract

Rights to access
and update the
distributed
databases where
the assets are stored

Access to internal & external (trusted third
party) data source(s) that triggers the
execution of terms

Source: Everest Group

Simply put, there needs to be a layer of business logic to merge data with the actions that people can take. Smart Contracts offer this layer of business logic, which enables blockchain to support a business process fulfilment. Smart Contracts manage transactions in a pre-programmed, automated way. The common logic used to complete a transaction is either 'If-this-then-that' or 'after-this-then-that'. Hence, it's a logic orchestration between subjects (or things) involved in the transaction. You can define the terms, the events and the signature needed to fulfill the process. If the product is not a tangible one, you can choose Digital Rights Management (DRM) to manage access or control the rights on the digital assets in the smart contract. Smart Contracts are decentralized and at the same time secured, executed in an automated way and don't need human intervention or paper trails. They are typically divided into two broad categories: Smart Legal Contracts and Code-Based. The Code-Based Smart Contracts, which are based on applications, can be further divided into three subtypes — DAO (Decentralized Autonomous Organizations), DApps (Distributed Applications) and IoT-combined contracts.

Types of smart contracts based on applications

Smart legal contracts

Smart contracts combined with legal contract templates

Decentralized Autonomous Organizations (DAO)

Multiple smart contracts combined with governance mechanisms

SMART CONTRACT

Distributed Applications (DApps)

Combination of smart contract codes

Smart contracting devices

Combined with devices (IoT)

Source: Everest Group

IoT-combined contracts refer to the use of smart contracts to govern interactions between physical devices on the Internet of Things. For example, a smart contract could be used to govern the exchange of data or the control of physical devices such as smart homes, smart cities, or autonomous vehicles. These contracts would enable IoT devices to operate autonomously, without the need for human intervention, based on the rules encoded in the smart contract.

The layer on top of those contracts, wrapping them up neatly with a bow on top, is 'code is law': the rules and regulations governing a digital platform or ecosystem are defined by the code that underlies it. In other words, the code that governs the platform is enforced automatically by the system, and users must abide by these rules or face the consequences, just as they would if they broke a law in the physical world. In the post-digital era, the concept of 'code is law' will become even more important as digital technologies continue to shape and influence every aspect of society. As more and more transactions, interactions, and activities are conducted online, the code that governs these interactions will become increasingly powerful and influential. In a blockchain-based system, the rules of the network are enforced by the consensus of the participants and the code that governs the blockchain. There is no central authority or governing body that sets the rules or has the power to change them. Instead, the rules are defined by the code, which is transparent and immutable.

A holistic example: Energy Communities

Let's end this chapter with a practical example that combines all Five Foundations: renewable energy communities. Rather than the traditional, centralized coal/gas/nuclear power station model of energy production, energy communities are a new model of community ownership and management of small-scale renewable energy resources. Such communities can be formed by a group of neighbors who decide to jointly develop, manage, and benefit from renewable energy projects such as solar panels, wind turbines, or biogas. This clearly represents a form of disintermediation as they bypass traditional energy companies and directly control their energy production and consumption. By decentralizing energy production and consumption, energy communities also increase energy resilience and reduce carbon emissions, contributing to the fight against climate change. While energy communities can leverage blockchain and smart contracts to enable secure and transparent transactions between producers and consumers, as well as automate the management and maintenance of energy systems. Notice that the consumer and producer in this scenario are one and the same — the 'prosumer' strikes again.

By using blockchain and smart contracts, energy communities can create a more democratic and secure system of energy management and exchange, leading to a more streamlined energy market, with reduced transaction costs and increased trust and accountability. Energy communities also incorporate the concept of personalization by allowing members to tailor their energy consumption and production to their individual needs and preferences. For example, members can choose to consume their energy or sell it depending on the time of day, weather conditions, or personal energy needs.

To deconstruct this idea further, let's consider one of the easiest ways to become an energy producer: installing solar panels on your roof. By connecting them with IoT devices that measure the outgoing and incoming currents through compensatory credit charges, you can exploit blockchain for your transactions. Now imagine if the people next-door and a few more down the street installed solar panels on their roofs, too. You now have many individual energy prosumers. But what happens when you or they are not at home and that energy is going back to the grid? If you and your network take collective action to form an energy community, via blockchain and smart meters you can calculate the energy consumed by the battery, the energy consumed by others in the network, and by each individual prosumer. You can connect the houses up into a mini grid with a smart contract. Then, you can monitor who used the energy when and who owes who. At the end of the month, you can consolidate your accounts. Using a smart contract, running on Ethereum for example (being typically more business process-focused than Bitcoin) you could connect several households with smart meters and batteries allowing for energy exchange between them, each compensated for the exchanged energy. This demonstrates the power of combining community and prosumer activity.

Such energy communities could see people as individuals come together and save the planet, bypassing the traditional holders of power – in more than one sense. I don't believe this is hyperbole. If we follow our political leaders and centralized energy companies currently, we will find ourselves in 2040 in a plus three degrees Celsius world. This is why it is important to assume an active role. The Post-Digital Society will focus on people, not hierarchy. We are the people, we are the power, and we want to control our freedom. And as we shall see in the next chapter, that will change society forever.

CHAPTER TWO

How society changes

The Italian Constitution was drafted in 1946 after World War Two, making us still a very young nation. The Constituent Assembly was elected by referendum (as was the abolition of the monarchy), and after 1 January 1948, when the Constitution came into force, we became a constitutional democracy. It was not possible to poll every person on every individual policy and law change, however. And so, as with all constitutional democracies, we created an election process to nominate delegates who act as our intermediaries and represent us in parliament. The parliament is merely the representatives of the people, and the people express themselves through their delegates. However, as we have learned, in practice this is not entirely true. While constitutional democracy has brought us many good things, such as freedom of expression and the right to vote, it has also brought negatives. Politicians increasingly concentrated on consensus and what people want in the short-term – something now known as 'Populism' – not on what the country actually needs. This can be damaging, as in the case of Italy's public debt, which – as I write – is the second highest in Europe at 145%. If we try to raise taxes to pay off this debt, there is a public outcry, and politicians are hesitant to act. In reality, they are not doing what needs to be done – they are simply trying to appeal to their base to win their vote in the next election.

The Post-Digital Society, for the first time since 1946, will offer us an alternative: direct democracy. In a direct democracy, citizens have a more direct say in the decisions made by the government because, in a very real sense, they *are* the government. Whereas now the people's representatives (politicians) dictate to the people, in a direct democracy it is the other way around: the representatives in government would no longer be politicians but rather civil servants whose primary role it is to enact the will of the people.

With the rise of digital technology, online voting has become feasible but not always safe and secure. In a Post-Digital Society, citizens could vote on issues directly through a secure, blockchain platform, the results then simply tallied and acted upon by the government. Everyone will have an immutable, fraud-proof digital ID, and their vote an equally immutable place in the chain that cannot be stolen or replaced. Town hall meetings could become more common, but with a digital twist. Using video conferencing technology, citizens could participate in virtual town hall meetings from the comfort of their homes. This would allow more people to participate in the democratic process, especially those who might not be able to attend in-person meetings due to geographic, financial, or mobility issues. Social media platforms too could play a role in facilitating direct democracy. For example, a platform could be created specifically for citizens to discuss and vote on issues. This could allow citizens to voice their opinions directly to their civil servant representatives and for their representatives to get a direct sense of the public's views on important issues.

There have already been successful, real-world trials, of this. In a Ted Talk given by Carne Ross, a world affairs expert who leads Independent Diplomat (ID), an innovative non-profit, he recounts an extraordinary Brazilian experiment in direct democracy:

> "Recently, direct democracy has been practiced by tens of thousands of people in a large city in Brazil called Porto Alegre, where thousands of people took part in debates to decide the priorities for the city budget. After 10 years of this, the World Bank, of all people, did a study of the results, and the results were extraordinary... If you include rich and poor alike in decision-making, the outcomes of those decisions are going to be more equitable, and sure enough, when the World Bank looked at Porto Alegre, they found that things like sanitation, healthcare, and education [became] much more fairly distributed than they had been before this experiment in participatory democracy began. They also found, interestingly, that both politics (the ugly form of partisanship) and corruption all

dramatically declined... if politicians are not allowed secretly to carve up a budget and pay off
their cronies, why do you need political parties
at all?"[19]

Critics of the Porto Alegre trial had expected anarchy, a
free-for-all – instead the experience was quite the opposite. No longer was it only the wealthy, the powerful, who
could get access to the decision-makers; now everyone was
the decision maker. I believe this possibility will finally be
realized for all of us in the Post-Digital Society, driven by
the normalization of decentralization and disintermediation discussed in the previous chapter. Decentralized decision-making could become more common, where communities are given more autonomy in decision-making. This
would, as in Porto Alegre, allow citizens to have a direct
say in the decisions that affect their daily lives.

As Lessig recognized in the early 2000s, the arrival of the
internet and personal computers gave us the technological
ability to introduce direct forms of democracy. What we
didn't have was immutable data. Voter fraud online would
be too easy. But following the advent of distributed ledger
technology, such as blockchain, we now have the ability to
achieve absolute data immutability. Blockchain is far bigger than just Bitcoin, but it was Bitcoin that proved the
concept: that a currency could be disintermediated from a
central bank. Before that, no-one thought it possible. Now
our right to vote can now be digitized too. For instance, an

NFT can be considered a form of digital right. By unifying blockchain, NFT, and digital ID technologies, as is already being done in Italy with electronic certified email, the platform for direct democracy is nearly complete.

We, as a people, can act directly in matters of governance, without the need to delegate our power through representative democracy. Through our computers and smartphones, we can read and vote on every deliberation and law, without intermediaries. Direct democracy empowers citizens not only to vote, but also to actively participate in the decision-making processes that shape our nation. It is feasible, right now, in 2023. The only barrier is the political will. Politicians are unlikely to vote themselves out of existence. It will take time. But at some point, a society used to disintermediation and decentralization in every other aspect of their lives, will simply demand it.

Collective leadership and Trilussa's chickens

According to the Italian poet Trilussa, "Statistics is the science according to which if you eat two chickens a day and I eat none, on average you and I eat a chicken a day." Trilussa's quote highlights the limitations of relying solely on statistics to understand society. In the context of leadership, if decisions are made by a small group of individuals with similar backgrounds and experiences, their perspective may not reflect the diverse perspectives of the population they serve. This results in decisions that benefit only a few, rather than the whole community, while using the (metaphorical) excuse "but look, the statistics say that everybody has a chicken!"

Consider direct democracy as the overarching, umbrella concept; 'collective leadership', meanwhile, refines it and makes it workable. Collective leadership offers the necessary alternative to the top-down leadership that is the current norm. In both business and politics, decisions are made from the top, including laws and regulations that affect such important issues as climate change, pollution, and fossil fuel transition. While we can all individually do our part to address these issues, it is not enough without leadership. For example, we have a clear need to transition away from fossil fuels, but our leaders struggle to take appropriate actions. They may claim to care about environmental issues but then sign bills to finance more coal extraction. We have seen many such lack of success by our leaders. These issues are apparent in many aspects of our lives, including the negative impact of high inflation and high energy prices. The UK, for example, is – as I write – experiencing an inflation rate of 10% to 11%, which is unthinkable. Imagine working hard for a year, and the next year your salary is worth 10% less. This may highlight the need for collective leadership.

Imagine a government detached from politics. This may seem unthinkable too, but it is of utmost importance. Under this model, we have managers who are not required to seek our approval, as they operate under a set of key performance indicators (KPIs) that are voted upon by us. The link between citizens and the government is established through three branches of power: legislative, executive, and judicial. For a true democracy to exist, these three branches must remain separate to maintain a balance of power. We currently only vote on the legislative branch, which then governs the other two branches. For instance, the parliament votes on laws proposed by the government, which could be a proposal for new funds. In a direct democracy the government issues a draft law, and citizens can vote on it without the involvement of parliament. In this way, the government executives act as managers who are hired by us, the citizens.

In a direct democracy, therefore, every citizen has a voice and a vote in the decision-making process. However, not everyone is equipped with the knowledge and expertise to make informed decisions on every issue. This is where collective leadership comes in. Collective leadership involves a group of people with diverse backgrounds and areas of expertise coming together to make decisions collaboratively. By pooling our knowledge and skills, collective leadership can help ensure that decisions are made with the best interests of society as a whole. This approach can ensure that decisions are made in a fair and equitable manner, as everyone has an equal say in the process. It is, after all, true democracy.

Furthermore, collective leadership can help to build trust and political engagement among citizens who currently feel disenfranchised; decisions are made transparently and with the input of the broader community. This can help to foster a sense of ownership and investment in the decision-making process, as citizens feel that their voices are being heard and that their opinions matter. Marina Gorbis, Executive Director of the Institute for the Future (IFTF), a nonprofit research organization, writes in her book "The Nature of the Future: Dispatches from the Socialstructed World" of the power of bringing many people with diverse backgrounds and points of view into the conversation:

> "For example, Foresight Engine, a game-like platform for collective foresight, developed by the Institute for the Future, ran a twenty-four-hour online idea-generating game for the Myelin Repair Foundation, which focused on developing drug therapies for multiple sclerosis patients. More than four hundred players- including corporate executives, teachers, engineers, students, and patients across five continents, as well as academic, government, and industry scientists-joined in generating more than three thousand ideas. They contributed, collaborated, and built on each other's ideas, creating value and receiving intrinsic rewards for their contributions. Clearly social media

platforms and tools are critical for communicating and transmitting data and information but also for establishing social connections in the group... As their ranks expand, biocitizens will leverage and trust what the group knows rather than rely only on experts."[20]

She goes on to write that, "The world in which knowledge resides only with individual authorities is giving way to a collective intelligence that emerges from the collaboration of many individuals creating and sharing information." I wholeheartedly agree. Collective leadership is essential for solving complex challenges in a rapidly changing world. The shift towards more distributed and networked forms of leadership will require new skills and mindsets, including the ability to collaborate across boundaries, to empathize with diverse perspectives, and to experiment and learn from failure. Gorbis's work suggests that the key to success in the 21st century will be the ability to embrace complexity, to adapt to changing circumstances, and to work collaboratively.

To return to Trilussa's chickens, collective leadership may not mean that everyone has a chicken – but everyone at least starts out with a real and equal say in their distribution. The group can draw on a wider range of experiences and perspectives, leading to more informed and equitable decision-making. By working collectively, individuals pool their knowledge, resources, and ideas to identify solutions that reflect the needs and values of the entire community, rather than just a few. Mass voting using electronic blockchain technology means that power is evenly distributed, and decisions are made collectively based on the votes of the majority. This system allows for a more inclusive and representative decision-making process, where the needs and interests of all members of society are law. We have moved from 'code is law' to 'the people are law'. The use of blockchain technology ensures that votes are transparent, tamper-proof, and immutable, thereby eliminating the possibility of fraud or manipulation. By leveraging the power of collective decision making, we can create a more just and equitable society, where everyone's voice is heard and valued. And, perhaps, where everyone does has a chicken (or the digital equivalent!).

Stakeholder capitalism

Stakeholder capitalism was first proposed by Klaus Schwab as a founding principle of the WEF. He outlined his thinking in a recent article 'Why we need the 'Davos Manifesto' for a better kind of capitalism':

> "'Stakeholder capitalism,' a model I first proposed a half-century ago, positions private corporations as trustees of society, and is clearly the best response to today's social and environmental challenges. Shareholder capitalism, currently the dominant model, first gained ground in

the United States in the 1970s and expanded its influence globally... hundreds of millions of people around the world prospered, as profit-seeking companies unlocked new markets and created new jobs. But that wasn't the whole story. Advocates of shareholder capitalism, including Milton Friedman and the Chicago School, had neglected the fact that a publicly listed corporation is not just a profit-seeking entity but also a social organism. Together with financial-industry pressures to boost short-term results, the single-minded focus on profits caused shareholder capitalism to become increasingly disconnected from the real economy. Many realize this form of capitalism is no longer sustainable."[21]

Attendees at the Forum's inaugural Annual Meeting signed the "Davos Manifesto," proclaiming a firm's principal responsibilities toward its stakeholders. The WEF, however, has arguably failed to live up to that premise since. Despite periodical proclamations, such as in 2019 by The US Business Roundtable, America's most influential business lobby group, that it would formally embrace stakeholder capitalism[22], very little has changed. It is the ethical equivalent of greenwashing. In fact, I challenge you to find a company that is *not* saying they are adhering to so-called 'ESG' commitments. They all *say* they are, and yet we are in an environmental, social and governance crisis. How can this be? The capitalist system has been structured around the interests of shareholders for decades. Shareholder capitalism emphasizes maximizing profits for shareholders above all else, leading to short-term decision making that can harm employees, customers, and communities. Additionally, the financialization of the economy, where profits are prioritized over long-term investments and innovation, has reinforced this shareholder-centric model. Rather than begin to overturn this, the rise of digital technologies has arguably cemented it even further, allowing for the emergence of new business models that prioritize shareholders – see, for example, the astronomic wealth of the likes of Jeff Bezos and Elon Musk.

However, it is my belief that the Post-Digital Society will finally make stakeholder capitalism a reality. The societal changes we've been discussing will have cascading impacts on our current economic models, especially shareholder capitalism — which continues to dominate the West. In a Post-Digital Society, stakeholder capitalism will become the dominant model because it better aligns with the values of younger generations who are increasingly concerned with social and environmental issues. As these generations come to hold more power and influence in the economy, they will drive the shift towards a more sustainable, stakeholder-oriented model of capitalism. Young people of course enter the business world as it currently is; it is unfair to expect them to change the fundamental economic models that have been in place for decades. However, there are several reasons to believe that the tide of stakeholder capitalism – a wave that has been slowly building since Schwab's proposal in 1971 – could yet become irrepressible. Younger generations have grown up in an era of increasing social consciousness and activism, and they are more likely to support companies that align with their values and beliefs. Schwab calls this "the Greta Thunberg effect", as the younger generation, of whom and for whom the teenage Swedish activist has been so emblematic, insists that the current economic system represents "a betrayal of future generations, owing to its environmental unsustainability"[23].

As Rob Walker, author of 'The Art of Noticing', with over 30,000 subscribers on Substack, argues:

> "For many decades, the primary stance of business has been to push for lower taxes and deregulation and the general sense that it simply didn't need government. This has had the net effect of weakening the social safety net: resistance to raising the minimum wage, little help for under-funded public schools, uneven access to health care – a drumbeat that has hit Black and minority communities particularly hard. As the Harvard professor Henderson points out, that has helped give young people a sense that the system is almost hopelessly rigged: Half of

Harvard Business School students surveyed, she says, professed to believe that 'capitalism is broken'."[24]

As with direct democracy, the digital age has created new possibilities for stakeholder engagement and transparency. With the rise of social media and other online platforms, stakeholders have greater access to information and a louder voice in shaping the behavior of businesses. This can lead to greater accountability and pressure on companies to adopt stakeholder capitalism. With the rise of disintermediation and decentralization, it's increasingly clear that a shareholder-centric economy may no longer be sustainable. The shift towards a more equitable economic model — one that benefits all stakeholders equally — is likely to become more pressing as these social phenomena continue to take hold. We have every reason to expect a future where technology is seamlessly integrated into our daily lives. As digital natives become the majority, we will see a significant shift towards a Post-Digital Society where all stakeholders expect to be heard in the drive towards social change.

Tokenization of society

Perhaps the best-known (and infamous) example of digital tokens is 'NFTs': non-fungible tokens. NFTs – so named to distinguish them from fungible tokens, which can be swapped – are simply a way to assign digital ownership rights. In fact, NFTs are implemented through a smart contract that utilizes cryptography. If you buy one unit of Ethereum, it is interchangeable, meaning you can sell it. Non-fungible tokens, on the other hand, cannot be exchanged but rather represent a unique right of ownership over a particular asset.

Tokens therefore encompass so much more than just NFTs. The real paradigm shift lies in 'tokenization' or 'tokenomics'. And tokenization/tokenomics is poised to play a significant role in the Post-Digital Society.

Tokenization involves the process of creating digital tokens that represent assets, such as real estate, art, or even individuals' time and skills. These tokens can then be traded, bought, and sold like any other asset, creating a market for these items that previously had no such market. Tokenomics, then, is the broader economic system that facilitates the use of these tokens. Tokenomics encompasses everything from the issuance of tokens to the management of the token economy. In the Post-Digital Society, the token economy could be used to incentivize certain behaviors, such as environmentally friendly practices, or to create a more equitable economic system. It also has the potential to democratize access to traditionally exclusive markets, such as real estate and art, by breaking down the barriers to entry and enabling anyone to participate in these markets. This will have a significant impact on the global economy, as it can help to redistribute wealth and create new opportunities for those who were previously excluded from certain markets.

The idea of tokenomics rewarding contributions to society, rather than just capital accumulation, will be driven by a number of actors, including governments and businesses, but also by society at large. Governments play a key role in implementing tokenomic systems that incentivize contributions to society. For example, governments could issue tokens to individuals or organizations that engage in socially beneficial behavior, such as volunteering, donating to charity, or engaging in environmentally friendly practices. These tokens could be used to access public services or receive tax incentives, creating a direct link between contributions to society and financial rewards. Businesses could issue tokens to employees or to customers who purchase eco-friendly products. These tokens could be used to access discounts, free products or services, or other rewards. Most importantly, however, communities can also play a central role, for example in creating a local token currency that is used to reward individuals who contribute to that community or local area. There is already a long history of local currencies for just this purpose, such as The Salt Spring Dollar in Canada, Bay Bucks in Michigan, or even the 'Seoul Love Gift Token' in South Korea. These do, in large part, act as a simple proxy to the national currency or dollar, with the benefit of boosting local economies and resuscitating ailing High Streets.

However, there are already signs of these shifting towards online currencies. In 2008 the Brixton Pound was launched in East London as a response to the financial crisis. Since then, over £500,000-worth of its colorful bank notes have been distributed, emblazoned with the faces of local heroes and even featuring guest designs from internationally acclaimed artists. However, in 2021 the decision was made to reinvent the Brixton Pound as a cryptocurrency, using the Algorand blockchain.[25] The press release stated:

> "Entering the third decade of the 21st century, the usefulness of paper money has started to recede globally, and the Brixton Pound now needs to become a digital Complimentary Local Currency. Tokenization via blockchain technology is the only platform to deliver this shift to "digital money" in a secure and trusted way... [with the] speed and security of the Algorand Permissionless Pure Proof-of-Stake protocol. In addition, the guaranteed finality of all transactions on the Algorand blockchain ensures that any payment made using a digital Brixton Pound will be fully complete and settled immediately (in under 4.5 secs to be specific)."[26]

It's easy to see how such tokens could rapidly become used to access local goods and services, creating a more self-sufficient and resilient community.

You might ask, how does this differ from old-fashioned money? Aren't bank notes simply a token that reward behavior? Aren't we just replacing one form of financial incentive with another? But as recognized by the Algorand-Brixton partnership, the practical mechanism for achieving this through the use of smart contracts can facilitate the issuance, distribution, and management of tokens. Unlike cash, smart contracts are self-executing contracts that automatically enforce the terms of an agreement, creating a transparent and immutable system for tracking the issuance and distribution of tokens. This system can ensure that tokens are issued to those who contribute, creating a more equitable and responsible economy. Tokens and money share similarities in that they both represent value and can be used as a means of exchange. However, tokens have unique features. They can be designed to represent a specific asset, such as property, art, or a share of a company, or represent ownership rights in a specific asset, which can then be traded on a blockchain platform. This also creates new possibilities for fractional ownership, making it easier for individuals to invest in assets that were previously inaccessible to them. A token could be used to access a particular service, or to reward specific behaviors, as we discussed earlier. This means that tokens can be used to create new systems of incentives and rewards that are not possible with traditional forms of money. In addition, being programmed with smart contracts, tokens can be designed to be more transparent, efficient, and secure than traditional forms of money. In short, tokens have unique features that make them a powerful tool for creating new economic systems.

Ethics and privacy: 'AI Who?'

Recently, I was thinking about AI ethics during a work meeting. One of my customers in Switzerland - Swiss Re - is one of the world's largest reinsurers, as measured by net premiums written. When I was asked to talk about the need to address AI ethics, I stressed that it's important to understand 'who' you're talking about when discussing this topic. If you want to talk about the machine and question *its* ethics, you're wasting your time. Machines can only perform the tasks they are programmed to do. To truly address AI ethics, we must talk about humans.

The same concept applies when discussing ethics in digitalization or any other paradigm. We must talk about human ethics and accountability. Laws and regulations must address people, not AI. It's the people who use AI software that must be accountable for their actions. When my clients ask me 'how do we control AI?', my response is always 'AI *who?*'

We already have frameworks for legislation on data privacy and cybercrime. We need to insert new amendments, where appropriate, for data privacy. For example, the government could issue a regulation stating that "probabilistic software cannot perform face impersonation in video." This is how we can make progress in AI ethics. I am also collaborating with the European Commission on this issue and again I stress the importance of addressing human accountability when discussing AI ethics. Even Mark Zuckerberg agrees. In an op-ed for *The Washington Post* in 2019, he wrote:

> "I believe we need a more active role for governments and regulators. By updating the rules for the Internet, we can preserve what's best about it — the freedom for people to express themselves and for entrepreneurs to build new things — while also protecting society from broader harms. From what I've learned, I believe we need new regulation in four areas: harmful content, election integrity, privacy and data portability... effective privacy and data protection needs a globally harmonized framework."[27]

Much of what Zuckerberg was calling for almost half a decade ago remains unimplemented. Yet it points to a viable path. Zuckerberg goes on to say that data shouldn't be stored locally; companies such as Facebook should be held accountable by imposing sanctions; and called for clear rules on when information can be used to serve the public interest and how it should apply to new technologies such as artificial intelligence. I agree.

Frank Pasquale, law professor at the University of Maryland

and the author of 'The Black Box Society', also argues that we need to focus on regulating the decision-making processes that underlie AI systems, which are often opaque and biased. But again, it is the human programmers who are 'opaque and biased', not the AI tool. We only get out of it what we put in. In particular, writes Pasquale, "Big data enables complex pattern recognition techniques to analyze massive data sets. Algorithmic methods of reducing judgment to a series of steps... also ended up firmly building in some dubious old patterns."[28] The RAND Corporation paper 'An Intelligence in Our Image: The Risks of Bias and Errors in Artificial Intelligence', undertakes the same line of enquiry, and argues that:

> "Automated learning on inherently biased data leads to biased results... [AI] algorithms try to extract patterns from data with limited human input during the act of extraction. The limited human direction makes a case for the objectivity of the process. But data generation is often a social phenomenon (e.g., social media interactions, online political discourse) inflected with human biases... This leads to the rather paradoxical effect that artificial agents, learning autonomously from human-derived data, will often learn human biases—both good and bad. We could call this the paradox of artificial agency."[29]

In short: new world, old problems. Rather than digitalization and AI offering us the freedom of objectivity, it is only as subjective or objective as the people and society that makes them. It will be important to establish guidelines that ensure that machine learning algorithms are used in a fair and equitable manner, and that they do not contribute to the marginalization of certain groups.

That said, I am very much a data privacy advocate. In a post digital society, the use of technology will only continue to expand and impact our daily lives in new and often unforeseen ways. As such, it will become increasingly important to establish ethical guidelines and privacy laws that are able to keep pace with these changes. One of the key challenges that will arise is the need to balance the benefits of technological innovation with the need to protect individual privacy. With more data being generated and collected than ever before, it will be critical to establish new laws and regulations that protect sensitive information from misuse or abuse. For example, there may be a need to limit the use of facial recognition technology or other forms of biometric data in order to protect individual privacy.

There will also be a need to establish new ethical frameworks that can guide our use of technology in a post digital society. This will require a deep understanding of the potential benefits and risks associated with different technologies, as well as a willingness to engage in ongoing discussions and debates about the ethical implications of our actions. The establishment of ethical guidelines and privacy laws will be critical for ensuring that technology is able to contribute to a better and more equitable world in a post digital society. This will require a collaborative effort between governments, businesses, and individuals, as well as a willingness to adapt and evolve these frameworks over time as new challenges arise.

Ensuring personal privacy in houses and buildings with multiple AI and IoT devices is one such example. But again, I ask: AI *who?* It is people that design and install devices. A simple approach is to implement privacy-by-design principles, where privacy is considered from the beginning of the product design process. This can include implementing strong security measures, limiting data collection to only what is necessary to perform the task at hand, and providing transparency and control for users over their data. Additionally, data encryption and secure data storage can help protect personal information from unauthorized access. Users should also be informed about what data is being collected, how it will be used, and given the option to opt-out of data collection if they so choose. Again, we have existing laws that can be used to cover this, such as the EU General Data Protection Regulation (or GDPR) which enshrines the right to say "no" to data collection in EU law.

Our existing governance and judiciary, laws, and regulations, need to – and can – keep pace with the rapidly evolving technology landscape, in order to protect individuals' privacy and prevent abuse of personal data. Governments can play a crucial role in setting standards for privacy and data protection and enforcing these standards through penalties and fines for non-compliance. Ensuring privacy in a post digital society will require a combination of technological solutions, legal frameworks, and individual awareness and responsibility – but these are rules for us, not for machines.

There is currently a concern about AI imagery and deep fake imagery – in the Post-Digital Society, how will we know what is real and what to trust? In early 2023, photos circulated on social media purporting to show Donald Trump resisting arrest. Another day, another fake: this time of Pope Francis appearing to take a stroll in a 'bling' white puffer jacket. The Influencer Chrissy Teigen tweeted to her 12.9m followers, "I thought the pope's puffer jacket was real and didn't give it a second thought. No way am I surviving the future of technology." At this point in time, Midjourney, DALL E2, OpenAI and Dream Studio are among the software options available to "anyone wishing to produce photo-realistic images using nothing more than text prompts", as CNS News reported[30]. But this is a problem that is easily solved: we will create an AI that recognize fake AI. AI can be used to authenticate news images as real or fake through a process called image forensics. This involves analyzing the image and its metadata to detect any signs of manipulation or tampering. AI algorithms can be trained to detect inconsistencies in the image such as inconsistencies in lighting, shadows, and pixel values. Additionally, AI can analyze the metadata of the image to verify its source and determine if it has been altered in any way.

An example of how AI is being used to authenticate news images is through the development of a tool called Veracity. Veracity is an AI-powered tool developed by the University of Maryland that analyzes news images and videos to determine their authenticity. It uses machine learning algorithms to detect signs of manipulation and tampering in the images.

One possible way to inform web users of the veracity of what they are seeing could be through an "authentication" stamp or label. This label could be embedded in the image itself or displayed next to it, indicating that the image has been verified as authentic by an AI system or human fact-checker. The label could also provide additional information about the image's source, date, and any other relevant context to help users better understand its meaning and significance, with information accessed by clicking on or hovering over the label. It's worth noting, though, that authentication labels alone may not be sufficient to combat misinformation and disinformation. We all must educate ourselves on how to critically evaluate sources and information, and platforms must take responsibility for monitoring and removing false or misleading content. Those battles are coming. But, while it might seem counterintuitive to some, it is a battle we want to enter into 'with' AI, not against it. Who are generating the fake images and videos? It is people, with the help of AI. It is with the help of AI then, that we too can solve these problems.

Globalization and populism

Globalization is, and always was, an inevitable consequence of the digital age. As Kofi Annan said in 2002, we either "help the outsiders in a globalized world out of a sense of moral obligation and enlightened self-interest, or we will find ourselves compelled to do so tomorrow, when their problems become our problems... In a world without walls, we can no longer think and act as if only the local matters".[31] While physical walls and national borders still exist, digital connectivity has already taken us global. As the English saying goes: the horse has already bolted. Those hoping to shut the stable door on globalization will find themselves forever frustrated.

The idea that democratic politics, national sovereignty, and hyper-globalization are incompatible was proposed by Dani Rodrik, a Turkish economist, at the start of this century. His theory states that it is only possible to have a maximum of two of those three elements at any one time. According to Rodrik, if we want to deepen globalization, we need to sacrifice either some sovereignty or some democracy, and vice versa. This concept, referred to as the "political trilemma of the world economy," did not receive much attention when Rodrik first introduced it in 2001. However, a decade or so later, it became relevant due to the struggles of the Eurozone crisis, Brexit, and the wave of populist politics sweeping the world. He elaborated in his 2012 book 'The Globalization Paradox':

> "Must we give up on democracy if we want to strive for a fully globalized world economy? There is actually a way out. We can drop nation states rather than democratic politics. This is the "global governance" option. Robust global institutions with regulatory and standard-setting powers would align legal and political jurisdictions with the reach of markets and remove the transaction costs associated with national borders."[32]

Rodrik admitted that it sounded "pie in the sky". But he argued that, "The appeal of the global governance model, however wishful, cannot be denied. When I present my students with the trilemma and ask them to pick one of the options, this one wins hands-down. If we can simultaneously reap the benefits of globalization and democracy, who cares that national politicians will be out of a job?" To which I would add, the benefits of globalization and *direct* democracy.

The current geopolitical climate between the US, Russia, and China is, however, having a significant negative impact on the concept of globalization. Globalization, which allows for production and sales anywhere, led to the deindustrialization of the United States, with many private companies moving their production to China for convenience. But China is now not only the world's factory but also the world's *brain*. This has led to the transfer of expertise and other necessary aspects of production to China, resulting in products being made at half the price compared to the US. Although the US is trying to reverse this trend and bring back production in the name of 'Build Back Better', it is challenging to do so. The end of globalization is something that is talked about, but it is contrarian to the progress we have seen so far. Globalization is a force for good that has shaped empirical and geopolitical relations, albeit now threatened by the tensions between the US, Russia, and China. But if globalization is shaped within the framework of stakeholder capitalism and sustainable progress, it will benefit the world. While the current model of globalization is exploiting the capacity of other countries, such as China, a union instead of globalization, stakeholder capitalism, and collective leadership could create a more inclusive and sustainable world.

This metamorphosis has also been referred to as Globalization 4.0. Globalization 4.0 is a term coined by the World Economic Forum to describe the fourth phase of globalization, which is characterized by the digitalization of the economy and society. This phase is driven by the rapid advancements in technology, particularly in the fields of artificial intelligence, robotics, and the Internet of Things (IoT). In Globalization 4.0, digitalization has transformed the way we live, work, and interact with each other. It has enabled new forms of connectivity and collaboration, breaking down barriers between individuals, organizations, and countries. The internet and digital platforms have made it easier to connect with people and businesses around the world. However, Globalization 4.0 also presents challenges and risks. The increased connectivity and interdependence have led to a more complex and volatile global economy, which can be vulnerable to systemic shocks and disruptions. The digital divide between countries and communities has also widened, with some groups and regions being left behind in the digital age. This again calls out for stakeholder capitalism and collective leadership: the engagement of all stakeholders in sustained dialogue will be required to draft a blueprint for a shared global governance architecture and warns that failing to adopt a new cooperative approach would be a tragedy for humankind.

Globalization has created a new reality in which we are all share interests and interconnected destinies. In this new reality, companies can operate in multiple countries, with supply chains that span the globe. Individuals can work remotely for companies located in other countries. And institutions, such as governments and international organizations, are increasingly working together to address global challenges such as climate change, poverty, and terrorism. Emerging technologies such as artificial intelligence, blockchain, and the Internet of Things are enabling new forms of global cooperation, in which individuals, companies, and institutions can work together to address global challenges and promote inclusive and equitable growth.

Globalization 4.0 is a recognition that no one country or institution can address global challenges on its own, and that we must work together to find new solutions that benefit everyone. This, of course, is grist to the mill of conspiracies that believe in a New World Order which wants to control us all. But here Klaus Schwab makes a distinction between the terms "globalization" and "globalism." According to him, globalization is a phenomenon that is driven by technology and the movement of ideas, people, and goods across borders. Globalism, on the other hand, is an ideology that prioritizes the global order over national interests. Schwab argues that the populist discourse often conflates these two terms and creates confusion. He suggests that while we are living in a globalized world, the question of whether all policies should be globalist is highly debatable.[33]

The rise of populist politics and anti-globalist rhetoric is often seen as a rejection of globalization. Some argue that this rejection is rooted in the perceived negative effects of globalization, such as job losses, economic inequality, and the erosion of national identity. These effects have been amplified by the emergence of the digital economy and the automation of jobs, leading to a sense of anxiety and insecurity among many people. It is, of course, important to note that globalization has also led to the creation of many new jobs and emerging industries, too, while also disrupting traditional industries. But it is worth considering whether anti-globalist rhetoric is actually a rejection of globalization or a reaction only to its negative effects. Populist politicians often tap into a sense of resentment among those who feel left behind by globalization and offer simplistic solutions to complex problems. They may blame globalization for these problems and promise to restore a sense of national sovereignty and identity, which they claim has been eroded by global forces. Yet the benefits are there to see, too, and will – I believe – ultimately win through. The rise of digital connectivity has enabled people across the world to connect and interact with each other in ways that were previously impossible. Social media, online forums, and other digital platforms have enabled people to share ideas, collaborate on projects, and connect with others from different countries and cultures. This will only increase. Even conspiracists like to engage with likeminded others across the world! After all, many of today's conspiracies could not have existed without digitalization and globalization.

As we will see in Chapter 5, the Metaverse has the potential to extend further beyond the physical world by using augmented and virtual reality technologies allowing users to seamlessly interact within real and simulated environments. We will all be global, and the question 'where are you from?' will soon appear old-fashioned. As a large multinational academic collaboration in the *International Journal of Information Management* put it in October 2022:

> "The potential impact on the way we conduct business, interact with brands and others, and develop shared experiences is likely to be transformational as the distinct lines between physical and digital are likely to be somewhat blurred from current perceptions... As the metaverse is parallel to the real world, more consumers will increasingly recreate the resemblances of their real lives in the digital worlds as they spend more time virtually. Status symbols such as digital clothing, cosmetics, household furniture, and jewelry will become significantly similar to real-world purchases and possessions. Therefore, it is likely that virtual possession will increase due to the replication of real-world habits."[34]

Physical barriers such as national entry restrictions may still limit our ability to travel and physically interact with people from other parts of the world. But our avatars will experience a freedom no previous generations have felt.

This creates a tension between the increasing digital connectivity and the limitations of physical movement. Therefore, it's essential to find ways to address the tension between digital connectivity and physical barriers, and to ensure that the benefits of globalization and digital connectivity are more widely shared. This requires a thoughtful and inclusive approach that takes into account the needs and all interests – again, a collective, stakeholder approach. In this sense, populist politics can be seen as a hindrance to progress. Despite claiming to be the opposite, populist politics is the death-throes of the old world order, writ large. But I don't think it is powerful enough to resist the inevitable, exciting internationalism of the Post-Digital Society.

Towards a new mindset

In her keynote speech at the Georgetown University Global Trade Academy in Washington DC, March 2023, Deputy Director-General of the WTO, Angela Ellard, said that the future of globalization will be determined by digitization. Against a post-pandemic backdrop where exports of digitally delivered services leapt up by 30% in 2021 compared to 2019 – she told delegates:

> "For years we have been hearing about the end of globalization (or de-globalization). But such a demise has been greatly exaggerated, to borrow from Samuel Clemens. Instead, the nature

of globalization is changing, and trade in intangibles, such as services, plays an increasingly important role. Trade in services will continue to increase as we enter the era of "the intangible globalization", a term coined by Norwegian officials. We also see potential in the digitization of trade through innovations like digital finance, customs edeclarations, and AI-assisted supply management tools."[35]

The societal changes brought about by the Post-Digital Society are, then, poised to transform economic models. The emergence of direct democracy and the growing importance of collective leadership will have a significant impact on the concept of stakeholder capitalism. As individuals and institutions navigate these complexities, there is a need to embrace technological advancements and promote a global mindset that recognizes our interconnectedness.

The rise of populist politics and anti-globalist rhetoric can also be seen in a different light; not necessarily as a rejection of globalization but rather a call for a more inclusive and equitable globalization that benefits all stakeholders. Rodrik's political trilemma of the world economy holds that democratic politics, national sovereignty, and hyper-globalization are mutually incompatible. However, with the right frameworks in place, we can move towards a more sustainable and inclusive globalization. The union of globalization, stakeholder capitalism, and collective leadership will be essential in creating a more inclusive and sustainable world. As we move towards this future, it may require us to rethink traditional political and economic structures, promote technological advancements, and embrace a more global mindset. By doing so, we can create a better world for ourselves and future generations.

In the next chapter, we will look at how this will bring about significant changes in the world of business, disrupting traditional business models and transforming the way companies operate. Businesses are likely to prioritize services over products, becoming ever more personalized to meet the changing needs of customers. At the same time, businesses will collect vast amounts of data on customer preferences, behaviors, and trends. While some of my views and predictions so far may have sounded socialist, or even communist, please don't misunderstand me: the Post-Digital Society is very much a capitalist one. And the opportunities to make a lot of money (or tokens, fungible or not) are very real.

CHAPTER THREE

How business must adapt

The patent for the first digital camera was applied for in 1977 by Eastman Kodak employees Gareth Lloyd and Steven Sasson. Their patent titled "Electronic still camera", filed on May 20th, 1977, and granted in 1981, described a camera that used an electronic sensor to capture and store images digitally, rather than using traditional photographic films. The camera converted the stored digital files into visible images on a display screen. The patent, which is still available to read online, even states: "As is well known, processed photographic film may not be reused. Recently, considerable effort has been given to the development of solid-state elements for imaging purposes. Such elements offer an advantage over photographic film in that, theoretically, they can be reused any number of times for imaging."[36] As we now know, this invention laid the groundwork for the digital camera industry, which revolutionized the photography industry. As we also now know, it spelled the end for Kodak. Because Kodak mothballed Lloyd and Sasson's invention and stuck to the pre-digital business model it knew best. The digital era subsequently swept the analogue era aside. And in January 2012, Kodak filed for Chapter 11 bankruptcy.

The Kodak story offers a clear parable for businesses now

entering the Post-Digital Society. Lloyd and Sasson did not have a direct means of communication with the CEO or top team. They spoke with their manager about the importance of patenting the technology for future advancements and received the funds to do so. However, the top executives at Kodak continued to give more emphasis to celluloid film and ignored the potential of digital cameras. When film sales started to decline, it was already too late – others reached the market first. If the management had adopted a collective leadership approach inspired by its employees, the future of Kodak could have been very different. In the Post-Digital Society, then, the successful company is one that applies a holistic, 360-degree view. The inability to adapt fast and change can cause a company to fail – not just lose a billion dollars but go bankrupt. This will happen to companies that do not apply lateral thinking. And, in my view, this will happen to hundreds, possibly thousands, of multinationals who do not adapt in time for the Post-Digital Society.

Stakeholder capitalism, not shareholder capitalism, will be the new value-creation model. It goes back to Trilussa's chickens: multiple stakeholders are more likely to make the right decisions, compared to a single (typically old and male) executive board. Technology can connect with stakeholders to create more appropriate KPIs, vote on business goals and translate them for suppliers, citizens, and for consumers.

Epochal changes don't announce themselves with fanfare. Instead, they creep up on us, subtly infiltrating our operations and upending our lives when we least expect it. That's why it's crucial to develop a nuanced understanding of the forces driving change — especially in today's world, where digital technologies are becoming invisible and ubiquitous. Instead of attempting to predict the future with absolute certainty, it's more beneficial to embrace a different mindset, one that's broad, inclusive, and fueled by lateral thinking. By taking this approach, you can prepare to face a range of challenges and opportunities, rather than trying to predict every detail of what's to come.

Many companies will benefit from the guidance of external consultants and advisors to support their strategic thinking. However, it's vital to take the further step of embracing internal collective leadership, i.e., to tap into the knowledge and expertise of your own human resources. In this post-digital world, the human being is *central*, and it's the employees who are the ones who live and breathe it every day. By tapping into their insights and experience, business leaders can gain a deeper understanding of the changes taking place and develop strategies that reflect their new reality.

Whether 'they' are employees, customers, or suppliers, it's crucial for business to rethink the role of people and reframe relationships in terms of sharing and respect. Doing so can help to foster a culture of collaboration, openness, and mutual support, qualities that are essential to building stronger, resilient, and ultimately successful organizations.

Collective leadership takes over the C-Suite

Decentralization is the driving force behind disintermediation. It seeks to distribute both power and functions previously managed centrally to broader levels of stakeholders. Just as it enables disintermediation from central banks in the financial sector, so in the constitutional context it paves the way for true democracy by and for the people. Direct democracy will mean empowering individuals to take control of the decisions that affect their lives, altering traditional power dynamics and reshaping the ways in which we approach governance and financial systems. So, what will this look like in the business world?

Collective leadership is the most important example. In a company, it is crucial to harness collective leadership because organizations and markets are increasingly complex. Enlarging your vision by involving various stakeholders, including employees and suppliers, is therefore essential. We already have exemplar business models here. Cisco provided an excellent example of collective leadership when they questioned why only top executives were consulted on certain issues. Several years ago, they conducted a company-wide poll to gather input from all employees on sensitive topics related to the workplace. The results were astonishing. Cisco's CEO John Chambers called the process "Cisco 2.0," which involved transforming the company's hierarchical management structure into a more collaborative and innovative one. One of the key components of this transformation was a shift to a more participatory decision-making process that involved employees at all levels of the organization. As part of this effort, Cisco launched an initiative called the "Idea Zone," or "I-Zone", which allowed employees to submit and vote on ideas for improving the company. The platform was open to all employees, and the top ideas were presented to the executive team for consideration. This helped to foster a culture of innovation and collaboration throughout the organization, and many of the ideas that emerged from the I-Zone were implemented, leading to improvements in areas such as customer service, product development, and efficiency.

The I-Zone initiative is often cited as an example of how a company can successfully transition to a more collective leadership model, and how involving employees at all levels of the organization can lead to better decision-making, innovation, and overall performance. Today, Cisco's leadership structure is still designed to encourage collaboration and teamwork, with a focus on shared decision-making and accountability. Business academic Craig Standing elaborated in a published journal paper: "In the I-Zone, other employees can comment or pose questions on the ideas. As a result, average ideas can trigger collaboration that can yield idea improvement or even better ideas. The ideas posted on the I-Zone are also kept on file for consideration at a later date. The success of I-Zone led Cisco to create I-Prize, a global innovation competition where $250,000 is offered to the best idea"[37].

In my consulting work I've seen another clear example of how the Post-Digital Society can increase social security by engaging citizens. By combining data from the National Institute of Geophysics and Volcanology (INGV) with information from citizens on their property structures, I helped to industrialize a patent for a mobile device that can calculate a building's risk of collapse. Essentially, the system combines a building vulnerability index with a risk factor related to the area's expected seismic events, as per INGV data. Through a mobile app — which uses AI to communicate verbally and increase accessibility — the citizen shares simple information about their building. In turn, the device auto-detects their location and immediately calculates the risk.

In Northern Italy, another organization with mixed public and private capital is combining computer vision and data to auto-detect poorly sorted or undifferentiated waste. Complementing this, citizens (through a computer system that uses IoT and mobile) can report any illegal landfills or identify the locations of ecological islands. More broadly, the app educates them on proper recycling practices and the impact their actions can have on the environment. As a whole, the system marries technology with the public will to improve waste collection and promote the reuse of materials. Ultimately, it shifts from the linear economy — i.e., take, make, and dispose — towards a green circular economy based on the principles reduce, reuse, and recycle. It also shifts from a top down 'do this' approach to one the engages and sources the skills and information from a far wider base than a company alone could hope to employ. By engaging external stakeholders, businesses ultimately have a far larger reach.

Stakeholder capitalism changes business models

In Europe, the German works council model is often upheld as the gold standard of employee representation. Within large German companies, a works council must be formed to represents the interests of employees, ensuring that laws and collective agreements are observed, employees' views regarding improving the workplace are implemented. This in turn sets collective agreements ("Tarifvertrag"), and arrangements between employers or employers' organizations ("Arbeitgeberverbände") which regulate the working conditions (i.e. working hours, wages, etc.). This is in addition to trade unions, which can be thought of as workers councils that span whole industries ad represent the interests of employees vis-à-vis employers and politicians for better working conditions, higher wages or more holidays.[38]

When people talk of shifting away from shareholder capitalism towards stakeholder capitalism, then, it is often workers councils and unions that come to mind. However, it is much more than that. Enabling and empowering employees is just a first step. Stakeholder capitalism recognizes the common interests of a range of *all* stakeholders. While return on investment for shareholders remains an important metric, it's not the only one that matters. In the Post-Digital Society, it's increasingly important to recognize the contribution of all parties who contribute to the success of a company. By doing so, we can foster a more collaborative, inclusive, and sustainable approach to business that benefits not only shareholders but also the wider community.

Shareholder capitalism, driven by the need to create shareholder value, has caused us to lose sight of why we are here. Our existence is not solely due to shareholders or to service their financial needs. Their investment is important and should be rewarded, and I'm not suggesting we eliminate shareholders altogether. That would be socialism or communism, which is a different concept. As a capitalist and entrepreneur, I am a shareholder in my own company and expect to be compensated for the risks I've taken with my money and work. However, over time, shareholders, like politicians representing our democracy, accumulate power. As their power and investments increase, as human beings, they start to ask the companies in which they own stakes to prioritize profit. Managers may feel pressured to prioritize profit at the expense of sustainability. This mentality disregards the environment and focuses solely on cutting costs to maximize returns. This is the negative outcome of shareholder capitalism: greedy shareholders.

On the other hand, are companies that operate independently from shareholders, such as co-operatives or social enterprises such as B-Corps. They recognize the importance of shareholders but also value other stakeholders. They prioritize workers' rights, better conditions, and consider the longer term needs of customers. They strive to sell environmentally friendly products, contributing to sustainability. They incorporate the planet into their production processes and invest in environmental protection. This approach emphasizes stakeholder capitalism, where prosperity is not limited to a few shareholders but extends to all stakeholders. Stakeholder capitalism does not lean towards communism or socialism; it is simply a logical approach that considers the interests of people, the planet, and prosperity.

After many years of unexpected market shocks, such practices contribute to the long-term viability and resilience of the business. Does this put off shareholders, who, remember, remain one very important stakeholder (albeit no longer the one with the 'veto' vote)? On the contrary, I would argue that it increases investor confidence and access to capital. As awareness of environmental, social, and governance (ESG) factors grows, investors are increasingly considering them when making investment decisions. Embracing stakeholder capitalism and demonstrating a commitment to sustainable and responsible practices can attract socially conscious investors. Companies that prioritize stakeholder interests are more likely to secure funding, have better access to capital, and enjoy higher investor confidence.

By considering the interests of all stakeholders, including workers and local communities, companies contribute to a fairer society. This can help alleviate social tensions and reduce the likelihood of social unrest or backlash against the capitalist system. When businesses actively work towards a fairer distribution of wealth and consider the interests of all stakeholders, it fosters a sense of social cohesion and promotes a more harmonious relationship between different segments of society. This approach not only benefits the stakeholders directly involved but also creates a more stable and sustainable society – and thus business environment – in the long run.

Rob Walker, author of The Art of Noticing, with over 30,000 subscribers on Substack, argues:

> "For business, the choice may become increasingly stark. The traditional bottom-line-only approach increasingly alienates workers and customers alike, appearing both callous and out of touch with a new reality. Companies that

demonstrate commitment to improving the social fabric — and thus contributing to the development of a more broadly robust worker and
consumer base — will attract the best talent,
the most customers. The business leaders who
build and expand will prevail over those who
retreat and retrench... This could be the surpri-
sing side effect of our current tumultuous era:
After years of airy talk, we could — we certainly
should — be on the brink of a new era in corporate thinking and behavior."[39]

If this sounds implausible, or only suited to smaller, niche business, consider the Danish pharmaceutical company Novo Nordisk. Novo Nordisk operates with a strong
commitment to stakeholder capitalism by prioritizing the
well-being of patients, employees, and the communities it
serves. The company focuses on providing affordable and
accessible healthcare solutions, particularly in the field of
diabetes care. Novo Nordisk invests in research and development, collaborates with healthcare providers and patient organizations, and implements sustainable business
practices. Novo Nordisk are one of several progressive
businesses that refer to this as The Triple Bottom Line:
combining a healthy economy, environment, and society.
This, they say, "ensures we manage our business sustai-
nably and pursue solutions that are in the shared interests
of the business and patients, and are in line with societal expectations."[40] To demonstrate its commitment to the

triple Bottom Line and stakeholder capitalism, Novo Nordisk is one of only four companies in the world that have incorporated it into the company bylaws – Social Impact, Environmental Responsibility, and Financial Performance must inform and guide every decision. This approach has led to social plaudits and recognition as a global leader in responsible business practices. But has this been good for shareholders? Let's let the sales figures speak for itself: Novo Nordisk revenue for the twelve months ending March 31, 2023, was $26.409B, a 13.54% increase year-over-year, and a 35.79% increase from 2019.[41]

Another example is Patagonia, the outdoor clothing and gear company. Patagonia has long been committed to stakeholder capitalism, emphasizing environmental sustainability, social responsibility, and employee well-being. The company actively promotes fair labor practices, uses recycled and environmentally friendly materials in its products, and donates a portion of its sales to environmental causes. Despite prioritizing values over short-term profits, Patagonia has experienced consistent growth and a loyal customer base, demonstrating that a stakeholder-focused approach can lead to business success while making a positive impact.

Moreover, Panasonic has been at the forefront of stakeholder capitalism through its GREEN IMPACT PLAN. Rooted deeply in its ethos is not just the creation of cutting-edge technology but also championing a society that's both environmentally conscious and sustainable. Through the GREEN IMPACT PLAN, Panasonic commits to embracing green technologies, enhancing energy efficiency, and slashing carbon emissions across all its endeavors. By forging alliances with local communities and global stakeholders, the company is sculpting solutions that are kind to the planet while propelling long-term sustainability. Much like Novo Nordisk and Patagonia, Panasonic perceives the crucial balance between profit, people, and the planet. This vision is not merely about financial prosperity but building a reservoir of trust and loyalty amongst its customers and stakeholders. Their stakeholder-centric approach has not only garnered accolades from environmental and sustainability factions but has also proven to be financially rewarding. Through the GREEN IMPACT PLAN, Panasonic underscores that a business can thrive economically while making a profound difference on the environmental and societal front.

The World Economic Forum White Paper, 'Measuring Stakeholder Capitalism', argues that the direction of travel now clearly favors a stakeholder approach:

> "The EU is revising its Non-Financial Reporting Directive, which seems likely to lead to more mandatory reporting on sustainability. IOSCO is looking at how to harmonize financial and sustainability reporting. The IFRS Foundation will soon begin formal consultations into bro-

adening its mandate to embrace sustainability issues... towards a comprehensive corporate reporting system that integrates sustainability reporting with mainstream financial disclosures... a core focus on ESG leads to improved corporate governance, more engaged employees and higher rates of return. Investors believe it is more important than ever to society, consumers, employees and shareholders that companies deliver prosperity in a way that respects people and the planet. This is no longer seen as a selfless crusade, it is at the core of sustainable value creation. There is clearly substantial momentum building..."[42]

By recognizing and valuing the full diversity of stakeholders, companies can navigate the complexities of the Post-Digital Society while fostering a more inclusive and sustainable economy. By actively seeking input from employees, customers, communities, and other relevant parties, companies gain diverse perspectives and insights that lead to collective leadership.

Decentralized Autonomous Organizations (DAOs)

DAOs are the next step – or giant leap – in this multi-stakeholder approach. The purpose of a Decentralized Autonomous Organization (DAO) is to encode an organization's operational rules into a computer program (smart contract). From a series of pre-set rules, DAOs allow users to digitize not only transactions but an organization's entire function. Smart Contracts therefore combine a legal template with a business logic, meaning that from their conception onwards DAOs are by nature decentralized, designed to be autonomous and self-governing, with decisions made by the members based on the rules encoded in the smart contracts. This can include DApps (Distributed Applications) that run on a decentralized network such as blockchain, designed to be transparent, secure, and resilient to censorship and cyber-attacks.

DAOs are not some imagined or speculated future business model. They already exist. I consult on two of them. The first is Busy DAO, founded in 2020 Prague, Czech Republic. A DAO designed for freelancers, unlike traditional online marketplaces managed by central companies, where the inner workings are unknown to its users, everything on Busy DAO is conducted transparently and digitally. Contracts are not signed or sent via mail, and money transactions are not physical. Instead, they exist as bits and bytes. Its website proclaims: "The emergence of DAO represents the logical progression in this digital evolution, which should have happened sooner" – and I agree.

The key distinction between a centralized organization and a DAO lies in the absence of a central authority that establishes the rules. While one can initiate the initial rules, they exist as smart contracts, written in code. Busy DAO serves as an example for freelance professionals, allowing them to create their own accounts and operate within an environment dictated by the community, not a central body. Any participant in Busy DAO can propose changes to the rules by creating a new smart contract, with approval requiring the consensus of 51% of the community. Once sanctioned, the smart contract becomes binding.

The significant difference compared to centralized platforms is that a DAO is not governed by a central authority; instead, it is run by the people within the marketplace. Users have the autonomy to create and modify their own rules. In contrast, on centralized platforms, users are passive participants and cannot propose rule changes. The term "autonomous" refers to the fact that smart contracts, being self-executing pieces of code, operate independently. Legal assistance is unnecessary; technical support is the only requirement to ensure the platform functions properly. The software and computers supporting the platform are ancillary.

Busy DAO's aim is to address the issues of centralization, low-quality offers, spam, and fees that plague traditional freelance platforms. By utilizing the BusyXChain blockchain and smart contracts, Busy DAO offers a proof-of-stake consensus mechanism. In particular, the decentralized nature of the blockchain allows every active user to participate and contribute to the network's security and throughput. One of the key features of Busy DAO is 'utility staking', which allows users to occupy platform space and earn rewards through staking their utility tokens (see tokenomics and tokenization in the previous chapter). By staking their utility tokens, users can earn a fixed reward of 33% per annum. These tokens also allow freelancers to create accounts and conduct transactions within the platform. Busy DAO's decentralized governance model also ensures that potential disputes and arguments are resolved by the users themselves. The outcomes are recorded on the blockchain, providing transparency and confidence in the resolution process.

Busy DAO ultimately aims to create a global decentralized platform that competes with centralized giants by offering exclusivity, quality services, and security: it's a heady mix which will appeal to a large number of people in the creator and gig economy. Clearly the technology developed by Busy DAO can be applied to other e-commerce areas through smart contracts, providing flexibility for future expansion.[43]

My second example is AgriUT, a DAO that operates as a nonprofit foundation. AgriUT's primary objective is to assist young farmers in developing countries by connecting them directly with customers. Let's say, for instance, there's a coffee farmer in Colombia. They want to showcase their coffee to potential buyers, so they ensure that the European company using their coffee places a QR code on the package. By scanning the code with a smartphone, customers can express their appreciation and support directly to the farmer. AgriUT facilitates exactly this interaction, allowing the consumer to 'tip' the farmer (you may have heard of 'buy me a coffee' – well this is more like 'thank me for *your* coffee'!). While AgriUT is a foundation, it functions as a permissionless DAO, embodying the principles of decentralization and autonomy. AgriUT enables people worldwide to tip and support farmers who are responsible for producing the goods, a disintermediation which eliminates the need for other intermediaries. Instead of sending money to an NGO and allowing them to decide who to help, individuals can personally choose and support specific farmers.

AgriUT also operates with a token system. The AgUnity Platform enables farmers to connect with suppliers, financial service providers, buyers, and other stakeholders, fostering economic opportunities for remote communities. The smartphone AgUnity SuperApp provides a marketplace for transactions, co-op management, blockchain-based supply chain traceability, and data capture capabilities. While the AgriUT token facilitates secure and cost-effective transactions within the platform while incentivizing positive behavior through tokenomics. But AgriUT's mission extends beyond rewards, aiming to reduce transaction costs, provide financial services, establish a digital marketplace, incentivize data collection, and stimulate economic activity within communities. Ultimately, AgriUT envisions the AgriUT token extending beyond its own platform, serving as a community payment token, and driving economic growth. It presents an innovative way to invest in social impact projects, circulate wealth transparently, and foster positive social and environmental impact through blockchain technology.

Both AgriUT and Busy DAO are notable examples of DAOs in action. They are real and operational, shaping the future of our society. While these are just two examples, it's crucial to recognize that as the number of DAOs increases—from ten to one hundred, one thousand—we are progressing toward a decentralized autonomous society (DAS). Tokens will be exchangeable and traded on digital marketplaces; their value ascribed by pure market value. I believe this shift is an inevitable future outcome. The decentralized autonomous society lies at the heart of the Metaverse, a topic we will explore in detail in Chapter Five. While the Metaverse harnesses virtual reality in the form of a mega video game, it also opens the doors to the society of the future — one that is shaped digitally and that functions via algorithms. Data and encryption will become markers of confidence, identity, and transparency. I see the Metaverse as the gateway to a gigantic set of interconnected, interoperable, and interdependent algorithms that will allow us to digitize our society and our economy from the very beginning.

Let's imagine other possible areas where DAOs could di-

srupt organizational models. In Italy we have a public automobile register, which is a database that contains all the
registrations and transactions relating to motor vehicles.
This register is managed by the Automobile Club of Italy
(ACI), an official body that aims to guarantee compliance
with the regulations set by the legislator. Since ACI officials do not have the right to change the rules — because
they can be changed only by legislators — it acts as an interface between citizens and a database. There are several
such organizations and government services. If the registry
were digitized with a DAO, we could radically streamline
administrative processes. By transforming legal rules into
smart contract clauses, we could allow citizens to register
independently, improving efficiency and eliminating the
bureaucracy associated with procedural flows. More broadly, if we combine DAOs in ways that satisfy the many
needs of citizens and businesses, we will see the birth of
a decentralized autonomous society (DAS): a cooperative
and interoperable aggregator of various decentralized and
autonomous organizations.

Decentralized Autonomous Society (DAS) is at core of the Metaverse

Research & infographic by Antonio Grasso

Digital Twins

The concept of digital twin is believed to have first been mentioned in the 1993 book *Mirror Worlds* by computer scientist David Gelernter. Today, it is commonplace in manufacturing. And the digital twin will further revolutionize all industries. A digital twin is an interactive graphic model representing physical assets' data. Picture a world where products are designed and developed virtually before physical production even begins, allowing companies to save costs, reduce time-to-market, and enhance product performance and quality. For instance, a hospital could consider the digital twin of a patient, where sensors monitor the patient's blood pressure and other vital signs and transmit that data to the dashboard. In the same way, an airplane engine can first be replicated on a computer, its engineers able to run thousands of simulations to predict possible scenarios. As Dr. Michael Grieves, a leading thinker on the subject, notes:

> "The digital twin is more than just a digital representation of a physical product; it's a digital model that allows companies to simulate, predict, and optimize the performance of that product in the real world. By creating a digital twin of a physical asset, companies can run simulations to identify potential issues before they occur, optimize performance, and reduce downtime. This technology has the potential to

revolutionize industries ranging from aerospace and defense to healthcare and smart cities."[44]

Repsol – the Spanish multinational energy and petrochemical company - now designs Automated Production Management (APM) and Integrated Flow Model (IFM) digital twins to improve the efficiency of assets and optimize production. By combining information from the workflows with various data sources, Repsol create a centralized tool where operators and engineers can quickly identify, classify, and trace opportunities for optimization. Guillermo Fernández Álvarez, Information Technology & Digitalization BP for Exploration & Production at Repsol, explains in his LinkedIn article:

> "One of the key components of Digital Twin is... autonomous and automated source of field optimization on real time, as all integrated flow models are loaded in the system and run to find the maximum output of our fields. Moreover, the tool calibrates and updates the model based on real data providing a real picture of the field... our Digital Twin technology is already deployed across all Repsol E&P operated-assets, comprising conventional and unconventional, onshore and offshore and a wide range of fluid characterizations and production methods."[45]

One area where digital twins will continue to shine is in

manufacturing optimization. These are virtual replicas of production lines, continuously monitoring real-time data to identify bottlenecks, streamline operations, and boost overall productivity. By leveraging these digital twins, companies will be able to unlock new levels of efficiency and revolutionize traditional manufacturing practices.

In my frequent collaborations with the market-leading data analytics multinational SAS, I've been given a front-row seat to the latest advances in manufacturing technology. At an event I attended, SAS introduced a groundbreaking concept called 'Modern manufacturing's triple play: Digital twins, analytics & IoT.' This trio represents the fusion of the tangible with the intangible, where digital replicas integrate seamlessly with real-time analytics powered by the Internet of Things. This synergy encapsulates the future of manufacturing, offering unparalleled insights and decision-making capabilities. With such tools at our disposal, the potential to transform industries is monumental.

But the power of digital twins doesn't stop at the production line. They are poised to reshape the way we approach maintenance and upkeep. Through real-time data analysis from sensors embedded in physical assets, such as machinery and equipment, companies can predict failures, schedule proactive maintenance, and minimize downtime. This predictive maintenance strategy not only saves costs but also extends the lifespan of assets, ensuring businesses run smoothly and efficiently.

Supply chain management will benefit greatly from digital twins. A virtual representation of the entire supply chain network, enabling companies to monitor inventory levels, track shipments, and optimize logistics in real-time, offers an accurate, real-time view of a supply chain. Businesses can mitigate disruptions, enhance customer satisfaction, and drive operational excellence. In the financial realm, digital twins can offer sophisticated modeling and risk analysis capabilities. By creating virtual replicas of financial systems and markets, companies can simulate various scenarios, analyze risk exposure, and make data-driven decisions.

When combined with AI – because the data is simply too much to manage for a simple algorithm alone – a digital twin can be used for smart city management, covering whole districts. Urban centers can create virtual replicas of their physical infrastructure to simulate and optimize resource allocation, energy consumption, and urban development. These advancements have the potential to revolutionize our cities.

As we march into the post-digital era, the digital twin signifies a transformative shift in how businesses operate and interact with their environments. From design and production to customer experiences and risk analysis, the applications of digital twins are vast and promising. Embracing this technology will unlock new levels of optimization, efficiency, and innovation, propelling industries into a future that once seemed unimaginable.

But perhaps the most intriguing application of digital twins lies in personalized consumer experiences. Imagine virtual replicas of individual customers, analyzing their preferences, behaviors, and needs, allowing businesses to offer tailored products, services, and recommendations. This level of personalization fosters customer satisfaction, boosts engagement, and cultivates long-term loyalty. The days of generic offerings will be replaced by hyper-customized experiences that cater to the unique needs and desires of each individual: also known as, 'personalization'.

Personalization: addressing the person, not the 'consumer'

In February 2019, Paul Daugherty, Accenture's chief technology and innovation officer, made the argument that, "By combining individualization with instant on-demand capabilities, businesses will be able to cater to individuals in every aspect of their lives, careers or business relationships—in effect, shaping their very realities." He, like me, recognized that we will soon enter the post-digital era, where we will see "a world where individualization and instant on-demand capabilities will make it possible for businesses to capture and deliver on momentary markets... The next wave of technology will make it possible for products, services and even people's surroundings to be deeply customized—and delivered instantly on-demand."[46] Dougherty emphasized the significance of personalizing interactions with customers, recognizing their value and the role they play in generating revenue. This is about the importance of people, specifically the concept of personalization. Many experts predict that Industry 5.0 will heavily rely on personalization, so companies need to adapt to this trend, or they will slowly but surely die out.

Personalization goes far beyond simply targeted advertising, already practiced by Meta on Facebook and Instagram. Imagine the concept of personalized medicine, which is being pursued in a collaboration between Siemens and the pharmaceutical company Pfizer. The current medical approach relies on standardized dosages based on average individuals, such as prescribing 800 milligrams of a drug. However, each person due to body shape and genetic inheritance may have unique requirements, with some needing only 600 milligrams and others needing 1000 milligrams. Unfortunately, current production methods do not allow for this level of personalization. To address this, Siemens and Pfizer are working together to establish a personalized supply chain. The process involves individuals undergoing medical surveys, with their age, weight, and blood analysis data being sent to the medical professionals. Based on this data, personalized medicines can be created without incurring extra costs. The digital technology plays a crucial role in collecting significant amounts of data needed for creating personalized medicine. The production process will be standardized, allowing for the incorporation of different components based on an individual's data set. Additionally, faster delivery methods, inspired by Amazon's same-day delivery, are being explored. Siemens is actively engaged in closing the gap between personalized medicine and home delivery, envisioning a scenario where patients receive their personalized medications after a hospital visit.

Such personalization extends beyond healthcare and can be applied to other products. Take something as everyday as shoes, for example. Currently, shoes are standardized. My shoe size in Italy is 43, but in some brands I'm 42 or 44. People's left foot can also be different from their right, for example. But now we have the tools to produce size 43.1, 43.2; if you send a picture of your feet with the scale on the side, artificial intelligence can measure every angle of my feet, transmit to the machine, and make the perfect shoes for my feet. This is something you already can do if you go to an artisan shoemaker and spend €1000. But with the advent of digital technology, personalized shoe production becomes feasible. By the rise of additive manufacturing, specifically 3D printing, offers new possibilities. The proliferation of 3D printing production centers worldwide will facilitate the manufacture of personalized items. Moreover, these will be complemented by faster circular supply chains, which will emerge to meet demand. These elements combined pave the way for personalized products in various aspects of life. The process is already underway, and the costs are expected to be significantly reduced compared to the current expensive alternatives. And the shoes won't cost €1000– they will cost €50.

This newfound manufacturing capability opens up a world of possibilities for the application of AI in creating personalized products across various domains. This capability not only pertains to production processes but also facilitates direct and personalized interactions with customers.

*

If Gareth Lloyd and Steven Sasson, those former employees of Eastman Kodak, were to emerge in a Post-Digital Society, they would have direct communication with a leadership team open to bottom-up engagement, perhaps via a Cisco-style I-Zone. They would quickly secure financing for product development, conduct proof-of-concept testing, and distribute prototypes to a thousand individuals (i.e. a wide range of stakeholders) for feedback. This was not feasible within the strict hierarchical structures prevalent in 1977. Business needs to learn humility to survive. The lesson is the need to relinquish the notion of supremacy, or the super-hero CEO, that ignores internal developments at all levels. We need instead, as we'll see in the next chapter, to understand disruptive technologies – and, where they provide genuine breakthroughs – embrace them wholeheartedly.

CHAPTER FOUR
Disruptive technologies

Albert Einstein's famous phrase, "we can't solve problems by using the same kind of thinking we used when we created them", could serve as a motto for the post-digital era. Innovative technologies will challenge, disrupt, and ultimately replace, traditional business models and old ways of thinking. Another quote often attributed to Einstein is: "creativity is intelligence having fun". In my view, the evolution from digital to post-digital was only possible because of our creativity, ingenuity, and desire to look beyond the status quo. The early iterations of the creator economy were, in many ways, human intelligence having fun.

In the coming Post-Digital Society, human intelligence will still be having fun, but it will increasingly be supported by computer intelligence, better known as AI. Much of the disruptive technology coming just around the corner will change lives, jobs, industries, and societies. It needs to be understood and analyzed in advance if we are to avoid foreseeable pitfalls and – where appropriate – embrace the positives. If we are to prepare ourselves for the changes to come, we need to enter with open eyes and minds, not closed ones.

We have discussed some of the key emerging disruptive technologies already, which underpin the central arguments of this book. For example, distributed ledger technology (blockchain) will transform business and government processes, opening up new ways of involvement from finance to democracy. We have seen how 3D printing will change the means of production through Servitization, opening up different business models by enhancing collaborative potential and hyper-personalization. But there are another Eight Disruptive Technologies that I want to give special focus to in this chapter: Generative AI; Nanotechnology; Advanced Virtual and Augmented Reality; Artificial Intelligence of Things (AIoT); Cybersecurity; Quantum computing; Edge Computing; and - which might raise some eyebrows, because it is not new, but we've only seen the beginning of its potential - Cloud Computing.

Generative AI

Today, we have 'narrow' AI, which can only perform specific tasks one at a time. For example, it can understand text, speech, or recognize objects through computer vision. But if we want AI to perform multiple tasks simultaneously, we need separate software programs dedicated to each function. Human beings by contrast possess general intelligence—a capacity for diverse thinking. We rely on our relationships with others to continuously generate our thoughts and ideas. Generative AI, therefore, operates on a similar principle. ChatGPT for example has the ability to learn and transform existing knowledge into something new – a process known as synthetic thinking. This transformation is an essential aspect to grasp amidst concerns about AI replacing humans or posing an existential threat.

First, let's take a step back to understand how generative AI was formed. ChatGPT did not emerge from nowhere. In 2013, variational autoencoders (VAEs) were introduced, becoming among the first deep-learning models to generate realistic images and speech. They allowed for the compression and reconstruction of data, but importantly also enabled the generation of variations on the original data. This ability to generate novel data sparked a series of innovations, including generative adversarial networks (GANs) and diffusion models, which further enhanced the generation of realistic, albeit synthetic, images. In 2017, Google's team introduced transformers, a landmark innovation in language processing, through their paper "Attention Is All You Need."[47] Transformers enabled parallel processing of words, learning their relationships and inferring meaning. This laid the foundation for modern large language models. In 2020, OpenAI released GPT-3 (Generative Pre-trained Transformer 3), a decoder-only model focused on generating text and predicting the next word in a sequence. With 175 billion parameters, it was one of the largest language models at the time. GPT-3 demonstrated remarkable capabilities in generating coherent and contextually relevant text, making it suitable for tasks like text completion, story generation, and even basic conversation. Lastly, encoder-decoder models like T5

(Text-to-Text Transfer Transformer) combine the strengths of both encoder-only and decoder-only models. They encompass a wide range of generative tasks while being more compact and computationally efficient than their decoder-only counterparts. All these advancements in generative AI and language models paved the way for the development of ChatGPT-3: from VAEs, encoder-only models, decoder-only models, and encoder-decoder models to a highly capable language model that can understand and generate human-like text and tasks.

Generative AI, then, operates by scraping human words and creations to generate 'new' outputs that exhibit distinct characteristics or novelty. Artificial intelligence cannot, however, truly generate something entirely new; it requires pre-training. Arguably, most humans spend their lives without original thought too, merely repeating their education, mimicking their upbringings, peers, and predecessors; we are all products of our society. The famous essay by French literary critic and theorist Roland Barthes, "The Death of the Author", argued much the same in 1967: authors were not, he suggested, creating new and original thought, but were merely (if you will allow me to extrapolate) the ChatGPTs of their age, consuming formal and social learning and spewing it back out in a new amalgamation of words. If Ernest Hemingway were born in 1799 or 1999, not (as he was) in 1899, would he have written the same series of novels in the same style? Of course, the answer is no.

Viewed this way, generative AI is not so dissimilar to humans; it uses the material/education it is given to synthesize human-like thinking into an artifact. It is worth noting that (at the time of writing this, in September 2023) ChatGPT's training data is collected only up until January 2022 – the data was then cleaned over a period of six months to ensure quality. The training phase involves feeding the generative AI with the cleaned data to create an artificial neural network. But very soon, generative AI synthetic thinking will become indistinguishable from human thinking. Indeed, in March 2023, numerous tech outlets including TechRadar, announced: "ChatGPT has passed the Turing Test".[48]

Undoubtedly, certain jobs will face disruption because of this. Tasks such as marketing, copywriting, translation, proofreading, and customer service are relatively straightforward for AI and will likely be disrupted. While it is crucial to acknowledge the impact on certain job roles, it is equally important to recognize the emergence of new jobs and opportunities. For instance, individuals required to feed data into AI systems, handle document sorting, serve as programmers to code and maintain AI systems or, perhaps more excitingly, to create. IBM's research lab blog, following the roll-out of ChatGPT versions 3 and 4 in early 2023, noted:

> "The last time generative AI loomed this large,
> the breakthroughs were in computer vision.

Selfies transformed into Renaissance-style portraits and prematurely aged faces filled social media feeds. Five years later, it's the leap forward in natural language processing, and the ability of large language models to riff on just about any theme... At IBM Research, we're working to help our customers use generative models to write high-quality software code faster, discover new molecules, and train trustworthy conversational chatbots grounded on enterprise data. We're even using generative AI to create synthetic data to build more robust and trustworthy AI models and to stand-in for real data protected by privacy and copyright laws."[49]

Many of these tools will free-up human time and creativity. Genuine human creative thinking will become more valued, not less. Again, AI is currently not capable of generating entirely new content. As McKinsey put it: "Generative AI outputs are carefully calibrated combinations of the data used to train the algorithms."[50] It appears new, therefore, but is not.

IBM's watsonx offers us a glimpse further into the future as generative AI advances. Watsonx is designed to multiply the impact of AI with three powerful components at its core. Focused on new foundational models, generative AI, and machine learning, the watsonx.ai studio is enabling AI to be fine-tuned to an organization's unique data and domain knowledge in previously impossible ways. A purpose-built data store provides the flexibility of a data lake and the performance of a data warehouse. It will enable organizations to scale analytics and AI workloads for all their data anywhere. This aspect of watsonx excites me because it means that organizations can leverage all of their data, regardless of where it resides, using a hybrid cloud architecture that provides the data foundation for extending AI deep into their operations. This gives us the concept of 'embeddable' generative AI: not just a tool, but a powerful ally. The age of the human isn't replaced by the age of the machine; rather, it is one of human and machine working together in symbiosis.

Nanotechnology

Nanotechnology will soon play an incredibly significant role in our lives. The nanoscale deals with dimensions between approximately 1 and 100 nanometers: the molecular level, where particles are so small that they can be injected into your bloodstream. This is an immensely important advancement in medicine and could see nanotechnology used to repair blood vessels or even the heart. *National Geographic* offer the following example:

> "One promising development in nanomedicine is the use of gold nanoparticles to fight lymphoma, a type of cancer that attacks cholesterol cells. Researchers have developed a nanoparticle

that looks like a cholesterol cell, but with gold at its core. When this nanoparticle attaches to a lymphoma cell, it prevents the lymphoma from "feeding" off actual cholesterol cells, starving it to death."[51]

Healthcare will clearly undergo a transformation. According to the Medical Device Network, "nanotechnology can be used to 'recognize' cells of interest. This allows associated drugs and therapeutics to reach diseased tissue while avoiding healthy cells". While the ability to control the release of a drug or therapeutic compound from its associated nanotechnology "is gaining a lot of interest from industry. This 'triggered' release, in theory, could be achieved from within the body."[52]

However, nanotechnology's impact extends beyond healthcare. Quantum dots, made of cadmium and sulfur, have been studied for uses in solar cells and fabric dye. Nanocomposites, combining nanomaterials with bulk materials, have applications in fields from packaging to thermal management. Nanomanufacturing techniques, building products atom-by-atom or molecule-by-molecule, hold amazing potential for microchip manufacturing. Graphene holds tremendous potential in the field of energy. Since graphene is just a single layer of carbon atoms connected in a hexagonal pattern, it is extremely thin and lightweight, and therefore an attractive material for nanotechnology applications. Assistant Professor Tzahi Cohen-Karni,

Researcher in Carnegie Mellon's College of Engineering, explained in 2017: "Imagine a self-sustained system, where the power is supplied to the nanosensing unit from 3-D graphene-based super capacitors. Someday we could have sensors that measure hormone or toxin levels, and you'd never have to replace the battery."[53] That 'someday' is a lot closer now than it was in 2017. The Australian author and Futurist Dr Mark van Rijmenam, and a big proponent of nanotechnology, writes:

> "Graphene-based batteries have also been developed to charge faster and last longer than traditional batteries. A great example is Samsung, which uses nanotechnology in its electronic devices to create more efficient and powerful microprocessors and memory devices. Samsung has developed a 10-nanometer FinFET technology for faster and more energy-efficient processing... Graphene's lightweight and strength [also] make it a promising material for the aerospace industry. It can be used to create strong and lightweight composites that can be used to make planes and spacecraft more fuel-efficient. Also, graphene-based sensors can be used to detect changes in temperature, pressure, and other conditions in spacecraft. NASA has developed a nanomaterial called aerogel, which is 95% air and is the lightest solid material in the world."[54]

The possibilities become endless when you imagine a world where tasks on a minuscule scale become achievable. Picture a robot that can bring together numerous nano-scale drones in a coordinated swarm. These could form holograms that allow you to see and interact with someone who isn't physically present, using metasurfaces, which are artificial structures engineered at the nanoscale to manipulate light. While this concept has been explored in science fiction movies, many companies are actively researching and developing micro machines that can aggregate light in just this way to form a singular representation. Imagine participating in a remote video meeting where the person appears in your room with you, and you can engage in physical interactions with them, all made possible through an instant formation of nano-machine swarms. Although this may seem unbelievable now, it may become reality. Nanotechnology holds immense potential to revolutionize various sectors, empowering us to accomplish feats that were once unimaginable.

Advanced Virtual and Augmented Reality

Augmented reality (AR) allows you to visualize how something looks against the backdrop of reality; whether that's Google Maps seamlessly added to your field of vision, or alternative redesigns of your living space presented before your eyes. AR enhances the reality by overlaying digital elements onto the physical environment, and it is already having a profound impact. In the business sector, training can be done by working together on the same task while wearing an AR/VR headset, even if we are in different locations.

Augmented reality will also allow us to interact with digital twins. The digital twins discussed in the previous chapter currently reside within computer screens; but with AR, they could be superimposed on the real thing (and with VR, we can fully immerse ourselves *within* the digital twin). Intelligent digital twins are being created too, infusing the capabilities of AI and digital technologies. In China, there are efforts underway to develop an intelligent digital twin of the entire city of Shenzhen. This shows the potential of the Post-Digital Society, where various aspects of society can be dematerialized and represented digitally.

In 2022, Google introduced a geospatial API that allows developers to create location-specific AR experiences by setting latitude and longitude coordinates. This API eliminates the need for physical space scanning and quickly determines the user's location by comparing images to Google Street View. Apple's ARKit 6, also released in 2022, brought enhancements such as 4K video recording during AR content usage, improved depth API for realistic scenes, motion capture from other people's movements, people blocking for virtual objects, and the use of LiDAR scanning for applications like RoomPlan, which creates floor plans.

Daniel D. Bryant, co-founder of Educators in VR and a

leader in the Virtual World Society, explained to the Pew Research Center that, "By 2040 the internet that you now access on a screen will be a *place* you can enter, visit and explore. Currently we are looking in through windows (literally), but we are soon going to be starting to climb *through* the windows and into the internet. The word web*site* implies a location. Currently this is mostly in 2D. What if these sites are in 3D and you can get in and interact directly...?"[55] As he goes on to ask, consider how creative people already get with content on the 2D internet; then add an extra dimension.

Andrew Makarov, Head of Mobile Development and an Augmented Reality Solution Architect at MobiDev, offers up the example of an AR partnership between Geenee AR and Ready Player Me: "By inserting your avatar into Geenee's WebAR Builder software, you can effectively 'wear' your avatar on camera. The software also takes into account cosmetic items on your Ready Player Me character, including accessories in the form of NFTs... Sotheby's, the fourth oldest auction house in the world, has begun offering AR experiences to bidders through an Instagram filter that allows them to see art up for auction up close and personal. Sotheby's used this technology to sell a painting for $121.2 million." Makarov also foresees AI and AR combining: "complicated algorithms must be used to make sense of sensor data of the environment. AI can simplify that process and make it more accurate than a model made exclusively by a human.... An app called SketchAR is an example of this technology in action. Users can freely draw in AR using this app. However, they can also use an AI to draw for them. The AI can create structures quickly. This shows that it's possible for AI programs to design objects in 3D space using the real world as the source environment. In the future, this may mean that AI will be able to design and create structures for use in the real world."[56]

How we will access AR and VR is also intriguing. Meta's mixed reality headset (project Cambria) is expected to offer high-resolution, full-color passthrough, giving users the ability to interact with virtual objects overlaid onto real-life environments. In other words, says Tech website Project-lint, "it is a VR headset that can offer a mixed reality (MR) experience. The MR features leverage Meta's Presence Platform, which was introduced in autumn 2021. Existing Quest headsets can only display passthrough content in grayscale, but Project Cambria has higher resolution image sensors"[57]. Apple Glasses could also make a comeback. So too could contact-lens-based AR. In June 2022, Mojo Vision Labs in Saratoga, California demonstrated its AR smart contact lenses, the Mojo Lens, that continuously track eye movements to ensure that AR images remain still as the eyes move. Information will no longer be at our fingertips but right before our eyes. Currently we are glued to the smartphone in our hands. But in the Post-Digital Society we will be wearing headsets or, more likely, lightweight smart glasses or contact lenses with advanced lens technology.

As we'll see in the next chapter, AR will also lead to extended reality (XR): an umbrella term for all immersive technologies including augmented reality (AR), virtual reality (VR), and mixed reality (MR). Elizabeth Hyman, CEO for the XR Association, founded by Meta, Google, HTC Vive, Microsoft, and Sony Interactive Entertainment to convene stakeholders for the development and adoption of XR, explains the evolution:

> "Virtual, augmented, and mixed reality are the gateway to phenomenal applications in medicine, education, manufacturing, retail, workforce training and more, and it is the gateway to deeply social and immersive interactions – the metaverse. Each day we're taking strides to make the technology better and ensure that the opportunities are limitless – because they are... XR technology will become the next major computing platform. Already, colleges and universities are teaching students in the metaverse. Human Resources professionals at companies like Walmart, SAP, Delta and many others are using the tool to train workers – some of the fastest-growing job categories in the U.S. are in industries that are rapidly adopting XR technologies."[58]

Artificial Intelligence of Things (AIoT)

The Internet of Things (IoT) typically evokes images of smaller objects such as smartphones or voice-activated smart speakers. But it extends far beyond diminutive gadgets. The autonomous car, for example, is a highly connected IoT: the network of interconnected devices and sensors embedded within the car, including cameras, lidar, radar, GPS, enable it to collect and exchange data with its surroundings. It is a 'thing', but it is highly connected. It is also AI: AI plays a crucial role in the decision-making and control systems of the autonomous car, processing the vast amount of data collected by the IoT sensors needed to recognize objects, predict behaviors, and navigate road scenarios. The convergence of these two key technologies: the Internet of Things (IoT) and Artificial Intelligence (AI) thus becomes: Artificial Intelligence of Things (AIoT).

Consider embedding AI capabilities into objects we interact with daily, be it a smartwatch, a computer mouse, or any other gadget. Such AI-infused devices could possess the power to anticipate our moves and needs, seamlessly remembering to remind us of upcoming meetings for example without relying on manual alarm settings. This augmentation of human-machine interaction holds transformative potential and will empower us all. Most of us have already experienced traversing an airport, moving effortlessly between terminals within a driverless train. Now, envision a train equipped with probabilistic software infused with probabilistic AI—an AIoT train. In this scenario, the train possesses cognitive capabilities, perceiving its surroundings through cameras, effortlessly adapting to environmental conditions without external intervention. Should passenger numbers dwindle or surge, the train can adjust its speed accordingly. This fusion of AI and IoT grants objects the ability to comprehend and respond, ushering in a new era of adaptability. Shivashish Jaishy, Engineer at AI company HEROZ, Inc., writes on LinkedIn that AIoT: "enables devices to learn from their surroundings and adapt, leading to enhanced intelligence and efficiency... In smart homes, AIoT-enabled devices can learn and understand individual preferences and habits. This technology automates tasks such as adjusting lighting, managing thermostats, and securing doors, thereby offering convenience and comfort."[59] Jaishy goes on to give the example of Siemens utilizing AIoT to optimize the efficiency of its wind turbines: by collecting data from sensors on the turbines, AI analyzes patterns to predict maintenance requirements, minimize unplanned outages, and increase the availability of their turbines.

The convergence of AIoT represents a paradigm shift that reshapes the way we interact with the world around us. By infusing cognitive capabilities into objects and enabling them to comprehend and respond, we transcend the limitations of traditional IoT, heralding a new era of human-machine interaction. By integrating AI capabilities into IoT infrastructure, cities can optimize resource management, enhance public safety, and improve overall efficiency. AIoT systems can monitor traffic patterns, predict and prevent accidents, optimize energy consumption, and even manage waste disposal. AIoT can enhance agricultural practices by enabling precision farming techniques, monitoring soil conditions, weather patterns, crop health, and optimize irrigation. It can even optimize energy consumption in our rooms, houses and across whole power grids, adjusting energy usage based on real-time demand, maximizing energy efficiency, and reducing costs.

As smart solutions provider Premio writes: "Global implementation of the Artificial Internet of Things (AIoT) is much closer than ever before; And one day it will be everywhere around us, seamlessly working behind the scenes improving people's lives and businesses without us even realizing it."[60] That, again, aligns with my definition of the Post-Digital Society. When everything becomes AIoT, just like tap water and electricity, it becomes the norm – expected, perhaps even underappreciated, but always there without us needing to think about it.

Cybersecurity

Almost daily it seems, our global news cycle runs stories about cyber-attacks. Whether it's stealing data or seeking ransom, these reprehensible acts make us feel, at best, insecure, and at worse, at the mercy of hackers. Of course, they also carry a significant cost to companies that must reclaim their data, restore public trust, and pay the penalty for violating privacy and protection laws. This is compounded when the data is considered 'sensitive' and isn't de-identified, as in the case of financial or health data. There is a highly sophisticated and lucrative market for hackers — one that's propped up on well-established business models, strategic operations, and extensive technological and human resources. As an executive and entrepreneur, I mitigate this by training employees to recognize the scale of the problem so that they can identify early warning signs. Globally, large tech players are innovating systems to make them less vulnerable to attack. For instance, the Zero Trust Security Model requires all users or devices — whether they fall within or outside an organization's network — to be authenticated, authorized, and continuously validated before they can access applications and data.

As everything becomes interconnected, we must acknowledge the risks of hacking and data privacy infringement. When we engage with social media in the digital era, we understand that our data will be exploited for advertising purposes. Advancements in innovation have provided us with platforms to express our creativity through social media, blogs, and videos, and we have eagerly embraced these opportunities. The pursuit of creative expression in the digital realm comes with challenges and compromises. Sharing one's creativity often involves sacrificing a certain level of privacy. In our quest for visibility and recognition, we have willingly exposed aspects of our personal lives and information. We must navigate the delicate balance between authentic self-expression and preserving privacy in an interconnected world.

However, privacy should not be conflated with cybersecurity. Mitigation for cybersecurity can only be achieved through preventive actions. For instance, Siemens adopts the concept of 'security by design', subjecting everything they produce to examination by an independent team to ensure it meets secure design standards. Additionally, other companies follow the principle of 'security by default', ensuring that products like the Alexa Echo device come pre-equipped with built-in security measures. When you install such a device, it is initially secure, but altering settings becomes your responsibility. Companies prioritize delivering devices with security by design and security by default to mitigate risks. However, complete avoidance of cyberattacks is impossible.

Joanna Bouckaert, the Community Lead at the Centre for Cybersecurity, considers what this might look like in 2030: "Public and private investments in security technologies, as well as broader efforts to tackle cybercrime, defend critical infrastructure, and raise public awareness about cybersecurity, are likely to reap tangible payoffs by 2030. Cybersecurity will be less about 'defending fortresses' than moving toward acceptance of ongoing cyber-risk, with a focus on bolstering resilience and capacity for recovery. As markers of this trend, passwords could be nearly obsolete by 2030, cybersecurity will be widely taught in primary schools, and cryptocurrencies will be more effectively regulated."[61] Cyber risks are not eradicated, then – unfortunately, far from it. But awareness of risk and safeguarding becomes integral to education and society.

Adopting security-conscious behaviors and staying vigilant, then – just as we do now, refraining from opening suspicious emails or clicking on dubious documents – will remain the basic tenets of cybersecurity. AI will, however, play a more prominent role in cybersecurity. Deterministic automation is cued to run a process based on some event or action: if this, then that. Such automation is reactive. Using this type of automation to identify anomalies in data flow or for continuous security updates is essential. Intelligent automation that learns from experience is used in integrated security not only to identify anomalies in data flow but also to resolve the problem. With virtualization, you need to put all the responses under the control of this intelligent software, which needs to be trained. It can identify anomalies, manage identity and access management, monitoring infrastructure 24/7.

As we have also seen earlier in this book, blockchain, being a decentralized ledger, allows us to securely store and transfer information – it is much harder for cyber criminals to compromise. We are already seeing blockchain becoming popular for applications that require high levels of security, such as finance, healthcare, and government – I expect this to move into personal and consumer applications, too.

However, there is a darker shadow that looms over any optimistic predictions related to cybersecurity: and that's quantum computing. As Miruna Rosca, cryptography researcher on Bitdefender's Cryptography and Artificial Intelligence team, warned in October 2021: "The underlying public key infrastructure (PKI) is built into every web browser in use today to secure traffic across the public internet... With their superior computational power, quantum computers will be able to break (or decrypt) public key encryption almost instantly.... adversarial nation-state or cybercriminal gang with access to quantum computing capabilities could access any and all communications and data encrypted using PKI."[62] Worrying indeed.

Quantum Computing

Quantum computing is not just disruptive, or (with all due respect to AR) a headset play-toy; it's a monumental leap forward in computer, and arguably human, evolution. Quantum computing is pushing the boundaries of imagination beyond what even I can fathom. As a programmer and software architect I can grasp the technical aspects, but still the sheer premise leaves me awe-inspired.

Traditional computing relies on processors, like the central processing unit (CPU) housed within your computer.

Visualize it as a cube, diligently performing one calculation at a time. Intel's creation of multi-core processors was a significant advancement in computing technology that involves integrating multiple CPU cores onto a single chip, allowing it to handle multiple threads and processes in parallel. Suddenly, computations could unfold simultaneously, drastically enhancing computational speed. But at the core of both the CPU and the multi-core lies transistors which perform calculations using binary digits, represented as 0s and 1s: the very definition of digital. Transistors are fundamental components of modern electronic circuits; its gates process binary signals and perform logical operations based on the binary representation of numbers, enabling the execution of various computations within a processor.

The quantum computer, however, is a fundamentally different beast. To truly comprehend it, one must delve into the realm of quantum physics. In quantum physics, the binary simplicity of zero and one disappears, giving way to the enigmatic 'qubit'. The qubit encapsulates a range spanning from zero to one, and every possible point in-between, a phenomenon termed "superposition." Picture an electron swirling within an atom—its precise location defies absolute certainty. Rather than stating definitively "the electron is here," we can at best surmise "the electron likely resides within one of these positions." It potentially exists simultaneously everywhere—a mind-boggling concept. Leveraging this superposition, a quantum computer can perform a vast array of calculations simultaneously, defying conventional computational limitations. Put another way, qubits can exist in a superposition of both 0 and 1 simultaneously. This property allows quantum computers to perform computations on multiple possible states simultaneously, vastly increasing their computational power for certain types of problems. Microsoft explains of its quantum computing Azure program:

> "[A qubit] can represent a 0, a 1, or any proportion of 0 and 1 in superposition of both states, with a certain probability of being a 0 and a certain probability of being a 1. Superposition allows quantum algorithms to process information in a fraction of the time it would take even the fastest classical systems to solve certain problems... It would take a classical computer millions of years to find the prime factors of a 2,048-bit number. Qubits could perform the calculation in just minutes."[63]

This remarkable proposition poses a colossal challenge for cryptography. Our current cryptographic systems operate under the assumption that breaking a password, particularly a complex one, would take years of computational effort. However, a quantum computer can do this within seconds, effortlessly exploring all possible states of a cryptographic puzzle and calculating every conceivable option in a blink of an eye. Herein lies the seismic shift—quantum computing is no longer deterministic like our standard 0-1 bit system, but rather probabilistic, governed by a realm of possibilities. Here, Professor Liqun Chen, head of the applied security group at the Surrey Centre for Cyber Security, University of Surrey, offers some reassurance in an article for *The New Statesman:*

> "... the US National Institute of Standards and Technology (NIST) asked for submissions for post-quantum algorithms in asymmetric encryption and digital signatures for standardization. On 5 July 2022, after three rounds of testing and review, the NIST announced the first group of four post-quantum algorithms selected for standardization. The NIST's choices of two lattice-based signature schemes and one lattice-based key encapsulation mechanism (KEM) scheme, along with a symmetric setting signature scheme, give the cryptographic community sound choices with which to begin the transition from today's cryptography to that suitable for the quantum age".[64]

The hardware required to achieve this is equally hard to fathom. Quantum computers do not rely on traditional binary transistors. Instead, they employ different physical systems, such as superconducting circuits, trapped ions, or topological qubits, to encode and manipulate qubits. This presents a significant barrier: the quantum computer requires ultra-low temperatures approaching absolute zero, around minus 200 degrees Celsius. Achieving superconductivity—a crucial component—exists only within this extreme temperature range, in highly controlled laboratories. Another significant hurdle is that the fragile, ephemeral nature of qubits has yet to be overcome – so far stabilized for only fractions of a second[65]. It isn't going to appear inside your laptop or smartphone any time soon, if ever. This also offers some reassurance to the cybersecurity question: no teenage hacker will have access to a quantum computer. Imagine, too, the fusion of quantum computing and artificial intelligence—the amalgamation that could birth an unimaginable form of general intelligence, beckoning one of the greatest challenges of our time.[ii]

Currently, it falls to tech giants like IBM and Microsoft to pour billions of dollars into quantum computing, surpassing their investments in artificial intelligence. And while still largely experimental, it is developing fast. In 2017, IBM unveiled a 17-qubit quantum computer; in 2022, just five years later, the Chinese produced a 66-qubit quantum computer 'Zuchongzhi 2.1', demonstrating that it could solve a problem in 4 hours that would have taken a state-of-the-art supercomputer 48,000 years[66]; in the same year, IBM unveiled a 433-qubit machine, with a stated goal to

---

[ii] In my opinion, quantum computing and AI should never be allowed to wed, but must remain separate tools. I'm not a believer in the 'singularity' concept, but combining quantum computing and AI would certainly be asking for trouble.

achieve 4,000+ qubits by 2025[67].

Quantum computing, whether used for good or ill, is the most disruptive technology in my list, with the most potential to transform our world. At IBM's 2022 launch, Dr. Darío Gil, Senior Vice President, IBM and Director of Research, announced: "[this] brings us a step closer to the point where quantum computers will be used to tackle previously unsolvable problems. We are continuously scaling up and advancing our quantum technology across hardware, software, and classical integration to meet the biggest challenges of our time, in conjunction with our partners and clients worldwide. This work will prove foundational for the coming era of quantum-centric supercomputing."[68] The very definition of 'digital' is the binary language of ones and zeros; quantum computing, then, is truly post-digital.

Edge Computing

Another disruptive tech that will grow in response to growing cyber risk, is edge computing. In contrast to conventional cloud computing, which allows software to be accessed from anywhere, edge computing represents a shift towards 'black box' computing. Amazon's Alexa is a prime illustration of edge computing. While it may not be explicitly labeled as "edge computing" on the box, it revolves around the concept of bringing computation closer to the source of data. Rather than relying solely on cloud computing, which operates remotely, Alexa processes numerous features and calculations locally. It is a black box, discreetly installed within close proximity, enabling swift responses without the need for data transmission to distant servers each time: that, in essence, is the definition of edge computing.

The growing use of edge computing is a recognition that not all data need to move to the cloud. For example, let's say you have a factory that produces a product using automation. Edge computing provides a proximity layer to the machines and then tries to give them the power to elaborate large amounts of data locally. If the data are being used only by the factory, the data don't need to go to the cloud. If you're thinking about an integrated security strategy, you need to include edge computing. For instance, imagine a military production facility that is working on a classified project involving the creation of new bullets. Quality control is crucial for each individual component, and the last thing you want is sensitive information leaving the confines of your factory. By utilizing edge computing, you can ensure that critical data stays within your premises, transmitting only aggregated figures and production totals to the cloud. This safeguards your designs and imagery from unauthorized exposure.

Edge computing could also be described as 'proximity computing', as it emphasizes the need for physical closeness in various scenarios. This requirement extends beyond simply enhancing data processing time, as witnessed in manufacturing where even a hundredth of a millisecond can significantly impact output. Edge computing combines the advantages of proximity, improved response times, and enhanced privacy. By embracing this transformative approach, people and organizations can achieve greater control over their data and ensure that it remains within designated boundaries. As the digital landscape continues to evolve, edge computing emerges as a powerful tool that empowers businesses to strike the delicate balance between efficiency and data protection. Premio, an Edge computing provider, explains:

> "Companies are shifting their computing workloads from the cloud to the edge to reduce the latency requirement to access the cloud. Edge architectures utilize edge computers that are deployed directly where sensors and IoT devices gather data. Being deployed right where the data is generated... allows local applications to run in real-time with incredible performance. Moreover, edge computing significantly reduces the amount of data sent to the cloud by filtering raw data before sending it away for additional processing; this process significantly alleviates bandwidth usage and saves workloads that require the resources of the cloud."[69]

On an individual and consumer level, edge computing presents less of a "gold mine" to cybercriminals, Dr Matthew

Schneider, assistant professor at Drexel University, told *Tech Monitor*: "an edge device with one student's data is less desirable than a cloud database with 1.2 million students' application records." You're certainly not going to enlist a billion-dollar quantum computer to hack a single edge computer. That said, edge devices may be easier for old fashioned burglars to steal and "physically access. And given their comparatively limited computing power, they may be less capable of security precautions such as encryption."[70] Edge devices are perhaps a double-edges sword when it comes to privacy – but finding the right balance of IoT, AIoT and edge computing will be a key challenge for the Post-Digital Society.

Cloud Computing

My description of edge computing perhaps makes it sound favorable to, or even the replacement of, cloud computing. But don't misunderstand me: cloud computing is not only here to stay, but it also provides the entire framework upon which the Post-Digital Society is built.

Cloud computing offers unparalleled scalability and flexibility, allowing businesses to easily adjust their computing resources based on demand. With the exponential growth of data and digital services, cloud platforms provide the infrastructure needed to handle these expanding workloads efficiently. The exponential growth of data necessitates robust storage and backup solutions. Cloud providers offer secure and reliable storage options, allowing businesses and individuals to offload the burden of managing their data infrastructure. Teams can work together in real-time, regardless of their physical locations, and easily access shared data and applications. This level of connectivity enables collaboration, streamlines workflows, and tap into diverse talent pools worldwide.

The emergence of edge computing may superficially appear to challenge the dominance of cloud computing, but in fact cloud computing is an indispensable component that enables Servitization, as we saw in Chapter One, where software applications are delivered as services. Servitization, particularly in the context of software applications, allows organizations to provide comprehensive services and solutions, driving efficiency and flexibility in the digital landscape. Cloud computing plays a pivotal role in enabling the delivery of these services, facilitating seamless integration and accessibility across various platforms. As long as the benefits of cloud computing continue to outweigh its limitations, it will remain a dominant force in the Post-Digital Society. In many cases, a combination of edge and cloud computing will likely be the optimal approach. Edge computing can cater to applications where proximity and real-time processing are critical, while cloud computing remains ideal for scenarios that do not need stringent privacy measures but require instant, easy sharing and access.

Nevertheless, the current geopolitical climate and the on-going battle for data control have introduced new concepts such as data sovereignty and data residency. These ideas emphasize the need for national boundaries and restrictions on data movement. For instance, if I am an Italian citizen, should I expect cloud providers to guarantee that my data remains within the borders of Italy? While the intention behind these initiatives may be rooted in safeguarding national interests, they risk reinforcing silos and impeding the free flow of data. This raises concerns regarding the fragmentation of the digital landscape and impediments to global collaboration and innovation. This is not, in my view a progressive step, but a regressive one.

In this rapidly evolving landscape, it is essential to find a balance between data privacy and the unrestricted exchange of information. Rather than erecting boundaries and clinging to data sovereignty, a more progressive approach involves breaking down barriers and fostering cross-border cooperation. Collaborative efforts among nations and organizations can lead to the establishment of robust frameworks that protect data privacy while enabling the global flow of information. Striking this balance requires open dialogue, international agreements, and a shared commitment to leveraging technology for the greater good.

The future of computing lies in a harmonious integration of edge and cloud computing, where each approach is strategically employed based on the specific requirements of applications. Cloud computing remains the backbone of our digital infrastructure, while edge computing introduces a new dimension of efficiency and privacy. By leveraging the strengths of both approaches and fostering international cooperation, we can navigate the complexities while maximizing the benefits for the Post-Digital Society as a whole.

*

When all the above are applied in a virtual Metaverse, where we can simulate any physical thing through its virtual representation by data, this raises even more questions – and forms the basis for the next chapter.

CHAPTER FIVE
People power: Web3 and the Metaverse

In Roman mythology, Romulus, twin brother of Remus and founder and first king of Rome, ends his mortal life via a mysterious transformation. During a sudden storm, he vanished in a cloud of darkness. The Senate declared that Romulus had ascended to the heavens and began to worship him as the god Quirinus, the divine protector of the Roman state[71]. The transformation of Romulus was more than a transition from man to God; it was a symbolic fusion of the earthly and the divine. It captures a yearning for transcendence that has resonated throughout human history.

Fast forward to the Post-Digital Society where people begin to interact within a digital universe; they become a part of it, transcending their physical forms to embody avatars and live out experiences that defy the limits of physical reality. Their Earthly, physical selves dissolve as they immerse themselves in a world where the boundaries between reality and virtuality blur. They become creators, controllers, and participants in a universe of their own making. This extraordinary possibility becomes a reality in Web 3.0[iii] and the Metaverse. And the seismic, tectonic shift it creates will surpass even artificial intelligence (AI) in reshaping our daily lives.

First, let's look at Web 3.0: the next evolutionary phase of the World Wide Web, it combines decentralization with user-centricity, ushering in a new era of online interaction. For this reason, Web 3.0 is often described as the "semantic web", meaning that it promises to revolutionize how information is structured and processed on the internet. The central goal of Web 3.0 is to enable machines to grasp the meaning behind user queries and respond intelligently, crafting a more personalized and immersive user experience. In contrast to the centralized nature of today's Web 2.0, controlled by tech giants such as Google and Amazon, Web 3.0 decentralizes data and distributes it across a vast network, giving users greater sovereignty.

The need for such decentralization is painfully apparent. In 2019, 43% of total net traffic flowed through Google (Alphabet), Amazon, Meta, Netflix, Microsoft, and Apple. According to WEF, this dominance is even more acute within their primary categories, with Google controlling

---

[iii] Author's note: Web 3.0 is also known as Web3 in the crypto world, but differentiating the two terms can be confusing for many, so let me state that Web3 and Web 3.0 have the same meaning. I know, Web3 is linked to the decentralized world and Web 3.0 to the semantic web. Still, we can consider them interchangeable, aiming for an intelligent and decentralized web and simplifying the understanding for many people.

almost 87% of the global search market and Meta reaching 3.6 billion unique users across its four major platforms (Facebook, WhatsApp, Messenger and Instagram).[72] Rebecca King, Engagement Lead, World Economic Forum, writes that Web3 aims to reclaim this space from big tech:

> "It is defined by open-source software, is trustless – doesn't require the support of a trusted intermediary – and is permissionless (it has no governing body) ... In a Web3 world, activities and data would be hosted on a network of computers using blockchain rather than corporate servers. The internet would likely have the same look and feel, at least initially, but your internet activities would be represented by your crypto-wallet and websites hosted through decentralized applications (dApps), digital applications run on a blockchain network... Anonymous single-sign-on will allow one username and authentication method across all websites and accounts, rather than individual logins for each site. This login would not require you to relinquish control of sensitive personal data."[73]

Aditya Raj, Senior Blockchain Consultant, Fujitsu Track and Trust Solution Center, goes a step further. He is not alone in claiming that the aim of Web 3.0 is no less than "to facilitate a fairer global economy". He writes:

"Web 2.0 ushered in the era of user-generated content... However, this internet is still centralized and governed by a shadow data economy that keeps data in siloes for competitive reasons. As dystopian as it may sound, corporations (the so-called Big Tech) utilize what users produce – valuable data – and sequester them due to its immense possibilities for capitalization. Web 3.0 however, may be the change we need to see for a future of fairness and transparency. The doors are open to a new era which will see power given back to the user, and by extension, communities all over the world. It will shift the opaque, shadow approach to data management towards a transparent and permissionless data economy capable of promoting true inclusion."[74]

I share this positive vision. As we have seen, blockchain allows trust and transparency to be infused into all activity on the web via its immutability and decentralized, distributed nature. As Raj goes on to say, "the internet will evolve from being an extractive economy where you're the product on centralized platforms such as Google and Twitter (renamed X), to one where as well as being a consumer, you're also a provider of services" – i.e.. the 'Prosumers' I identify as a foundational pillar of the Post-Digital Society in Chapter One.[75]

At the core of Web 3.0 then, as with so much of the Post-Digital Society, lies the principle of decentralization. Unlike its predecessor, where data is concentrated within the grasp of a few dominant entities, Web 3.0 leverages innovative technologies like blockchain to facilitate data distribution across a decentralized network. This decentralized approach liberates users from the shackles of standardized interfaces designed for the masses and empowers them with newfound control over their digital existence.

User-centricity therefore permeates the fabric of Web 3.0. Powered by AI and semantic technologies, Web 3.0 attunes itself to the individual user, grasping their intent and preferences. This allows for a highly tailored and personalized user experience, setting Web 3.0 apart from the more generic interactions of its predecessors. Additionally, Web 3.0's use of smart contracts (remember 'code is law' - self-executing agreements written into code) paves the way for advanced user-machine interactions, enabling seamless, secure, and transparent transactions. Meanwhile, decentralized autonomous organizations (DAOs) can be established to democratize decision-making based on the quality or volume of a user's interaction on site or decentralized app (dApp).

As with any transformative technology, the timeline for Web 3.0's mainstream adoption remains uncertain, contingent upon the maturation and widespread acceptance of foundational technologies such as AI, blockchain, and

semantic web technologies. Nevertheless, compelling real-world applications are already surfacing. Decentralized Finance (DeFi) serves as a prime example, leveraging
blockchain, particularly Ethereum, to build a financial
ecosystem devoid of intermediaries like banks or brokers.
Platforms like Uniswap, Aave, and Compound enable
users to lend, borrow, and earn interest in a decentralized
manner, bypassing traditional financial institutions. DeFi
developers and product teams have the flexibility to build on top of existing protocols, customize interfaces, and
integrate third-party applications. For this reason, DeFi
protocols have been termed "money Lego". Lex Sokolin,
Global Fintech Co-Head of ConsenSys, has claimed, "We
are a stone's throw away from the global financial industry
running on a common software infrastructure."

Ethereum-based games have also become a popular use
case for decentralized finance because of their built-in economies and innovative incentive models. PoolTogether, for
example, is a savings lottery that enables users to purchase digital tickets by depositing the DAI stablecoin, which
is then pooled together and lent to the Compound money
market protocol to earn interest. ConsenSys lists the main
benefits of DeFi as:

- Programmability.

- Immutability.

- Interoperability.

- Transparency.

- Permissionless.

- Self-Custody.[76]

It goes on to offers the examples of Crypto wallets like MetaMask, Gnosis Safe, and Argent which help to interact with decentralized applications to do everything from buying, selling, and transferring crypto to earning interest on your digital assets.

A braver new world

If this smacks of Utopianism, then perhaps it should. Consider the name 'DeFi': it is not merely an abbreviation of two words combined but pronounced as 'defy' its aim is to defy and overturn the centralized financial system.

The decentralized ethos of Web 3.0 also finds expression in decentralized social networks like Mastodon, which enables users to host their servers, granting them ownership and control of their data, thereby breaking free from the clutches of centralized control. Non-Fungible Tokens (NFTs) further showcase Web 3.0's ability to revolutionize digital ownership. Utilizing blockchain technology, NFTs represent unique digital assets, such as digital art and virtual real estate, ushering in a new era of secure and transparent digital interactions.

Web 3.0's journey towards realization is underpinned by the fusion of technological advancements and regulatory frameworks. Blockchain and distributed ledger technology serve as the backbone of data decentralization, while encryption and privacy technologies safeguard sensitive information. Regulatory aspects can complement this, setting guidelines to protect user data and privacy. The European Union's General Data Protection Regulation (GDPR) for example offers data protection, granting users data access rights, and mandating informed user consent. In a Web 3.0 environment, such regulations may adapt and evolve to extend these protections while navigating the unique challenges presented by the decentralized nature of Web 3.0.

Web 3.0 will mark a clear departure in the role that each of us will have to play in a Post-Digital Society. As I mentioned in my opening chapters, disintermediation and decentralization will serve as the catalytic seeds of change, placing us as individuals more prominently on the economic scene. One way this could work is peer-to-peer (P2P). When we currently access the web, our computers use the HTTP protocol in the form of web addresses to find information stored at a fixed location, usually on a single server. In contrast, a decentralized Web3 could find information based on its content, meaning it could be stored in multiple places at once. The tech academics Edina Harbinja and Vasileios Karagiannopoulos elaborate:

> "... this form of the web involves all computers providing services as well as accessing them, known as peer-to-peer connectivity. This system would enable us to break down the immense databases that are currently held centrally by internet companies rather than users (hence the decentralized web). In principle, this would also better protect users from private and government surveillance as data would no longer be stored in a way that was easy for third parties to access."[77]

As the authors go on to note, this harks back to the original premise behind the internet and Web 1.0, first created to decentralize US communications during the Cold War to make them less vulnerable to attack.

By further providing individuals with the opportunity to use their skills and talents to create content and earn a living, the creator economy running on Web3 has the potential to democratize work and break down traditional barriers to success. However, this shift will require a collective effort to create a responsible and sustainable system that benefits everyone, not just a select few. As we look ahead to the Post-Digital Society, it is clear that we must embrace this new economy with a commitment to collaboration and building a shared community.

Entering the Metaverse

As Web 3.0 blossoms and active user participation takes center stage, online users become dynamic contributors rather than mere consumers of digital content. Extended reality (XR) will be the tool that empowers us to co-create and shape our shared virtual space. This is the Metaverse: a persistent and interconnected digital universe akin to a giant, global video game, where we are represented by avatars. This is where, like Romulus, we enter a cloud and emerge transformed. The Metaverse will span a vast array of activities, from socializing and entertainment to work, education, and commerce, via an ever-evolving digital ecosystem. And it won't only be gamers who enter – it will be all of us, almost every day.

The term "Metaverse" was initially coined by science fiction writer Neal Stephenson in his 1992 book, "Snow Crash." He has since explained of his initial concept, in an interview with *Vox*, that:

> "The metaverse itself, I think, is kind of neutral. The first parts of it that we see are kind of garish. And people are playing violent games and there's lots of ads and tacky crud there. It's the first thing that meets the eye when you go

into the metaverse. But it's also made clear that there are people... who have put a huge amount of effort into making extraordinarily beautiful, detailed houses that they can live in in the metaverse."[78]

Needless to say, Stephenson's idea would have a huge influence on the minds of many young soon-to-be Silicon Valley tech billionaires.

The term 'meta' also brings to mind metaphysics, a branch of philosophy that explores the fundamental nature of reality, including the relationship between mind and matter, substance and attribute, and potentiality and actuality. This connection to metaphysics is apt, as the Metaverse represents a new dimension of reality, a virtual world that exists beyond the physical yet is fundamentally tied to it.

It's crucial to understand that, unlike Stephenson's fictional creation, there won't just be one monolithic Metaverse. There can be multiple Metaverse, each with its own rules, physics, and economy, like different websites today. Users might have other avatars in different Metaverse just as we currently have several usernames, and items purchased in one Metaverse may not work in another. As Diana Ambolis explains in *Blockchain Magazine:*

> "Metaverses offer unique virtual possibilities, much as each social media network offers its

customers unique options. As a result, each metaverse serves a particular purpose within the larger metaverse... some metaverses might focus on gaming while others might focus on gatherings or concerts... Axie Infinity, Decentraland, and SecondLive are three examples of cryptocurrency metaverse initiatives that each take a different approach to metaverse development."[79]

Despite their differences, the underlying principles of user control over data, security and trust provided by the blockchain, and intelligent interactions facilitated by AI, remain the same and unite these diverse Metaverse under the broader umbrella of the single Metaverse concept. In essence, the Metaverse offers an immersive digital platform where people can interact in real time, not just with each other, but with an environment that responds and evolves. This transformative technology provides a new dimension of interaction, bringing us closer to a world where physical and digital realities begin to blur, or at least coalesce.

The concept began to gain significant attention in 2021-2022, driven by Facebook's rebranding to 'Meta' and societal shifts prompted by the COVID-19 pandemic which necessitated remote interaction in digital workplaces. This surge stimulated new investments amounting to tens of billions of dollars. Nick Clegg, President, Global Affairs at

Meta, wrote in a Medium post that "the Metaverse is a logical evolution. It's the next generation of the internet — a more immersive, 3D experience." However, he was keen to stress that it went beyond the "detached worlds of VR, where we don headsets that take us out of our environment in the physical world and transport us somewhere new. VR is one end of a spectrum. It stretches from using avatars or accessing Metaverse spaces on your phone, through AR glasses that project computer-generated images onto the world around us, to mixed reality experiences that blend both physical and virtual environments."[80]

While the media was gleefully quick to diagnose the 'death of the Metaverse' in March 2023 when a Mark Zuckerberg investor call scaled back Metaverse investment and piled more into AI instead[81], it's clear that it was already bigger than – and no longer reliant on – just one company. Just a few short months later, Apple released its new Vision Pro AR headset – its "most ambitious product since the iPhone"[82] – viewed as key hardware for Metaverse interaction, and the Metaverse buzz was back. Nike has filed trademark applications for downloadable virtual goods, Walmart revealed plans to build online retail stores stocking virtual merchandise, while virtual real estate has already sold for hundreds of thousands of dollars. In China, Shanghai public authorities plan to offer public services through the Metaverse. Indeed, some Metaverse environments have already launched, such as Horizon Worlds, which presents a social environment for networked friends to socialize, and Horizon Workrooms, which brings professionals together in a collaborative digital workspace.[83]

When the Pew Research Center and Elon University's Imagining the Internet Center asked over 600 technology experts to share their insights on the Metaverse in 2022, 54% said that they expect by 2040 the Metaverse "will be a truly fully immersive, well-functioning aspect of daily life for a half billion or more people globally". One participant, Elizabeth Hyman, CEO for the XR Association (founded by Meta, Google, HTC Vive, Microsoft, and Sony Interactive Entertainment) gave a number of interesting real-use cases:

> "Virtual, augmented, and mixed reality [collectively known as XR] are the gateway to phenomenal applications in medicine, education, manufacturing, retail, workforce training and more, and it is the gateway to deeply social and immersive interactions – the Metaverse... Already, colleges and universities are teaching students in the Metaverse. Human Resources professionals at companies like Walmart, SAP, Delta, and many others are using the tool to train workers – some of the fastest-growing job categories in the U.S. are in industries that are rapidly adopting XR technologies. Uses of XR include warehousing and inventory management, product engineering and design, immer-

sive job training and upskilling and virtual health care patient monitoring. Particularly in the
health care setting, we're seeing XR use with
children. For example, the Children's Hospital
Colorado is using XR to help to change the pe-
diatric hospital experience for the better – for
instance, for distraction and pain management
reducing the need for anesthesia and physical
therapy."

Daniel D. Bryant, co-founder of Educators in VR and a
leader in the Virtual World Society, similarly predicted,
"By 2040 the internet that you now access on a screen
will be a *place* you can enter, visit, and explore. Currently
we are looking in through windows (literally), but we are
soon going to be starting to climb *through* the windows
and into the internet. The word web*site* implies a location.
Currently this is mostly in 2D. What if these sites are in 3D
and you can get in and interact directly, rather than with
a keyboard and a mouse? Think how creative people already get with creating and monetizing content on the 2D
internet. Now add a third dimension..." (Not that everyone
agrees. Justin Reich, associate professor of digital media
at MIT and director of the Teaching Systems Lab, called
the Metaverse "a dystopian hellscape where a completely
financialized world is stripped of any culture and value.")[84]

A common pushback is, "haven't we been here before?
What about Second Life?" While Second Life created a si-

milar buzz by making many of the same claims in the early 2010s, it was an idea whose time and technology was
yet to come. One of the distinguishing characteristics of
the Metaverse is that it exists continuously, regardless of
whether individual users are present or not. This contrasts
with virtual worlds like Second Life, which depend on the
active participation of users. Second Life was also a single,
stand-alone virtual world, whereas the Metaverse – like
the Web – is envisioned as a vast collection of interconnected spaces and experiences. It will include systems for
decentralized finance, cryptocurrency transactions, smart
contracts, and digital ownership through Non-Fungible
Tokens (NFTs). And perhaps most importantly, in contrast
to solitary virtual worlds that are managed by centralized
entities (like Linden Lab for Second Life), the Metaverse
is envisioned as a largely user-governed and decentralized
space. This decentralization empowers users to have more
control over their experiences, and through collective decision-making, they can shape the rules and norms of the
Metaverse.

For his part, Mark Zuckerberg unveiled the science fiction
side of the Metaverse — a virtual world where users can
interact, game, and experience things as they would in the
real world. But conceiving of the Metaverse as nothing
more than a large social media platform fails to appreciate how it could change our social, political, and economic
order. The Metaverse represents a significant leap forward
from former virtual worlds or games. By fostering intercon-

nectivity, persistence, economic complexity, interoperability, immersive experiences, and decentralized governance, it has the potential to create a more dynamic, engaging, and expansive digital landscape. At its core is blockchain technology that could pave the way towards a decentralized autonomous society. The blockchain's inherent transparency and immutability reduce friction and foster trust between parties that do not know each other directly. This opens the door to a non-discriminatory ecosystem where everyone can participate in an autonomous, transparent, and inclusive production system.

Far from creating a state of anarchy, this model allows us to become global citizens with our digital identity and enable us to create economies without the need for intermediaries. More than a fascinating thought experiment, decentralization is a lever that, when pulled, could give way to unprecedented changes for our social and economic order, and ultimately lead us to "direct democracy".

Metaverse: the business case

The transformative potential of blockchain, cryptocurrencies, Web 3.0, and the Metaverse extends into societal structures and how we interact. It also breathes new life into business models, providing opportunities for growth and innovation. A key emerging concept is the Industrial Metaverse. Imagine for example a digital twin of a physical factory that allows for virtual testing and optimization of processes within the Metaverse, connecting virtually the whole factory ecosystem, including all the stakeholders. McKinsey have already imagined it, and paint the following picture:

> "... nearly every aspect of work can take place solely digitally or, at the least, before it does so physically. Immersive experiences, enabled by augmented (AR) and virtual reality (VR), will allow employees to gain real-world product design experience and training from their desks as they manipulate 3-D digital replicas of equipment... The journey toward the enterprise metaverse, while still aspirational, has already begun with the development of the engines that will power it: digital twins. Imagine this future in the enterprise metaverse: A digital version of your end-to-end supply chain, from raw materials to delivery, continuously replicates in real time."[85]

The benefits of digital twinning on the Metaverse are multiple: when a component from the new supplier has been chosen, the R&D organization receives a 3-D replica of it, and its impact on customers and existing processes is automatically simulated. The virtual factory also simulates any resulting production disruptions and gives leaders recommendations by optimizing workforce and shipping schedules. In retail, a virtual retail store could proactively send store managers recommendations for updating store layouts and product lines to fill any temporary gaps on shelves. Then there are possibilities that we can't even yet imagine, as McKinsey contemplates: "As implementations mature, leaders will want to shift from simply replicating what exists today to digitally reengineering entire processes and experiences... The enterprise metaverse offers an opportunity to reinvent these experiences and processes in a digital context."

The Industrial Metaverse can also be understood as a convergence of IT (Information Technology) and OT (Operational Technology), enabling seamless interaction between data processing systems, the machines on the factory floor, and all the other partners involved. This digitized universe brings a variety of new opportunities for businesses in different scenarios. The Metaverse can be used for safe and efficient training of employees through meta-representations of actual work environments. It provides the ability to simulate before executing or delivering, such as using a digital twin to simulate a machine's behavior, thereby speeding up setup times and avoiding unforeseen production issues. Furthermore, the Metaverse can facilitate tasks for remote users. Through augmented or mixed reality, experts can operate from a distance, eliminating the need for a physical commute.

Additionally, the Industrial Metaverse dovetails with the concept of servitization, where products traditionally sold as items are now provided as services. Many businesses will transition from selling physical products to providing comprehensive services on the Metaverse. Such platforms will increasingly allow businesses to reach global consumers directly, leading to more efficient operations, increased margins, and a better understanding of customer needs.

One intriguing symbiosis is the potential integration of the Industrial Metaverse with 3D printing. A manufacturing company can utilize third-party design services in the Metaverse, and then produce the artifact directly where it is needed through industrial 3D printing service centers. This integration could significantly speed up the product development cycle, reduce waste, and allow for more customization, offering a glimpse into the future of manufacturing in the Post-Digital Society.

Ultimately, the Metaverse has the potential to enrich human experiences and enable greater access to information, opportunities, and connections. There are potential pitfalls, however, that we should be aware of if we are to avoid them. As the Metaverse grows in sophistication and becomes more immersive, some may choose to live primarily in the Metaverse – drawn to the idea of a digital existence that offers boundless possibilities. This could come with real-world health and mental health implications. Conversely, there will be individuals who prefer to remain firmly rooted in the tangible physical world, who prioritize face-to-face interactions, but begin to miss out on the employment and financial possibilities of the Metaverse (imagine being without the internet for a day, a week, a month – how long would your career and finances stay healthy?). This could result in a societal divide, with some individuals investing the majority of their time, resources, and identity in the Metaverse, while others retain a more traditional lifestyle. Such a two-tier society raises questions about potential disparities in access to opportunities, resources, and societal benefits between distinct groups. As the Metaverse's influence grows, policymakers and communities may need to address these potential disparities proactively.

The Metaverse could also potentially lead to distinct groups, new elites and inequalities within the virtual realm itself. As with all technological advancements, the potential for a digital divide is significant. Those with better access to advanced hardware, the latest headsets, reliable internet, and digital literacy skills will be better positioned to benefit from the Metaverse. Conversely, individuals or communities lacking such resources may find themselves excluded or disadvantaged, leading to a tiered society based on digital access and literacy. The ability to purchase virtual real estate, premium avatars, advanced equipment, or virtual goods and services could become a new status symbol, distinguishing the virtual 'haves' from the 'have-nots'. In a virtual economy where real-world money can buy advantages, new forms of economic disparity can arise. If the Metaverse ends up being controlled by a handful of powerful tech companies, it could result in a further concentration of power and influence. These companies could potentially shape the Metaverse in ways that serve their interests, leading to monopolistic practices, privacy concerns, and undue influence over the rules and norms of the Metaverse.

Privacy remains an issue to be ironed out, too. The International Association of Privacy Professionals (IAPP) tackled this issue in its blog, stating:

> "Users' personal data will be at particular risk of exploitation given the vulnerabilities involved when data is ported from one metaverse to another... European users of a metaverse operated by a U.S. company may thus exercise their rights under the GDPR. In the metaverse, that EU data subject may be in a virtual nightclub with a Japanese citizen and a California resident. Physically, all can still be in their homes, each subject to a different privacy regime. Privacy law has not quite caught up to state and international boundaries yet, and it's years away from reaching a consensus on the choice of privacy law in the metaverse. This is likely to generate complex conflicts between the requirements of the regulations from differing jurisdictions, i.e., data breach notification requirements. Therefore, it's tempting to include

a "privacy law selection clause" in terms of service of the particular metaverse."[86]

While these are all potential issues, however, they are not inevitable outcomes. Proactive measures such as inclusive design, robust regulations, decentralized governance, digital literacy programs, and affordable access can play a key role in ensuring that the Metaverse becomes an inclusive and egalitarian space rather than a new frontier for societal divides. There is ongoing research and debate in these areas, and many believe that with the right approach, the Metaverse could be a powerful tool for promoting equality and expanding opportunities. Instead of viewing the Metaverse as a divide, society could embrace it as an opportunity to expand human connections, knowledge sharing, and creative expression. Striving for a sustainable society that values inclusivity, empathy, and a sense of shared purpose will be vital in navigating the complexities and potential challenges presented by the integration of the Metaverse into our lives.

The Metaverse could also contribute to real-world reductions in material and energy consumption, potentially leading to a net-zero carbon world. If a significant number of people opt for virtual remote working instead of a physical commute, it could drastically reduce greenhouse gas emissions related to transportation. Additionally, virtual workplaces would decrease the need for physical office space, reducing energy consumption related to building, heating, cooling, and maintaining these spaces. The Metaverse could even usher in a new era of digital goods, which require no physical materials or energy to produce and transport, unlike their real-world counterparts. Fashion is one industry where this could have a significant impact, which currently has a substantial environmental footprint. We may need to fly less to achieve of travel wishes, able instead to explore boundless online worlds. And our real-world experiences will likely become more local, contributing to the local economy and social cohesion, not detracting from it. If we spend more time locally, we will want our neighborhoods to be greener, more pleasant places to live. The Post-Digital Society, then, has the potential to be a greener, cleaner, low-carbon world. And that's what I'll explore in the next (and penultimate) chapter.

CHAPTER SIX
Sustainability and the Post-Carbon Society

Every morning at dawn, I walk in an urban forest, a green oasis in the heart of Naples. This daily ritual allows me to appreciate the splendor of nature, which in turn inspires reflection on the importance of preserving our environment – not only for the planet's well-being but also for our health, wellbeing and survival.

Growing up surrounded by nature had a significant impact on me. I was raised in an agricultural environment. My parents weren't landowners but workers, earning a meager income from their hard work in the fields. Even at a very young age, perhaps one or two, I was often with my parents in the fields because I was too young to be left at home. The cycle of moving with the seasons was a part of our life back then. When I was around six or seven years old, circumstances required us to relocate to the city. Yet the memories of my early years spent in close contact with nature remained vivid in my mind. I recall the sensory details – the sounds, the light, the feeling of the water – it all carved a niche in my soul. Even now on my walks, when I encounter similar sensations, like hearing birds chirping or witnessing the wind rustling the trees, it triggers those deep-seated memories and emotions within me. I believe these reactions are a legacy of my parents' connection to agriculture and nature. Despite the challenges, those early experiences with nature have profoundly shaped who I am today, and I suspect they have a significant influence on my current path.

There's no denying that the early digital revolution contributed to climate change and habitat loss, from mining materials to producing e-waste. However, I believe that a Post-Digital Society has the potential to mitigate these problems, provided we adopt sustainable practices in our use of technology and resources. Empowered by technology, we will have greater control and responsibility over our actions and how they impact the environment and society. The key is understanding our power and the difference we can make.

I believe this heightened sense of responsibility could be a wake-up call to those who aren't currently motivated to strive for environmental and social sustainability. The realization that our individual actions can directly affect the health of our planet and our society could encourage more people to change their habits and behaviors. In addition, technology will continue to provide us with new ways to reduce our consumption of materials and resources. From digital solutions that reduce the need for physical products to advances in renewable energy and recycling, a Post-Digital Society offers opportunities to achieve a more sustainable future. The challenge is to balance our technological advancements with our commitment to sustainability and to use this balance to drive positive change.

As I return from my dawn walk, my thoughts change as I leave the forest and drive to my office. Along the way, I encounter scenes of homelessness – makeshift tents dotting the urban landscape, an all too vivid reminder of our society's social challenges. At a stoplight, a stranger approaches to clean the windshield of my car, an act both simple and profound in its implications. In these moments, the importance of expanding our understanding of sustainability becomes crystal clear. Sustainability is not just about the environment, but also the social and economic. In the Post-Digital Society, the pervasive influence of technology on all three elements of sustainability will become undisputable.

The "3 Ds": Digitalization, Decarbonization, and Decentralization

Over the course of writing this book, I've come to the conclusion that sustainable progression – and indeed the future production of clean energy – is fundamentally reliant on the "three Ds": digitalization, decarbonization, and decentralization.

The concept of decentralization as we saw in Chapter One refers to distributing power to individuals and communities, enhancing the capabilities at the local or peripheral levels, rather than its reference in blockchain technology.

This shift towards decentralization is also paramount in the field of energy, particularly during this period of energy transition where we are witnessing a significant transformation from analog processes to a digital landscape. This transition embodies a cyclical exchange from physical to digital mediums and vice versa, creating a loop of seamless communication. For instance, local energy communities. Similarly, concepts like the Metaverse, web 3.0, and blockchain technology are echoing this sentiment by providing more autonomy and power to the people.

We are at a juncture where the other two "Ds", digitalization and decarbonization, can steer the course of this energy shift. They mutually benefit one another. Therefore, to successfully navigate the energy transition, we need to critically evaluate our strategies to ensure they are not adversely influenced by elements distant from science or environmental welfare. The crux of the matter lies in recognizing that true decentralization can only be achieved by redistributing power to the grassroots level. This, in my opinion, forms the central theme of our ongoing discourse, enhancing individual and community empowerment.

Ultimately, the balance between digital progress and sustainability is in our hands. We need a holistic approach that considers all aspects of our environmental impact, from material consumption and travel habits to the energy that powers our digital world. The responsibility for creating a sustainable Post-Digital Society rests with all of us, and it is our actions and choices that will determine the future of our planet.

As we have seen, 3D printing hubs, or even home machines, will replace the need to ship and fly products around the world. Currently, according to *Quartz*, "By weight, 40% of maritime trade consists either of fossil fuels on their way to be burned or of chemicals derived directly from fossil fuels."[87] Reducing the need for such shipped goods will greatly reduce global emissions. 3D printing and additive manufacturing will therefore significantly change how we produce and distribute goods, with promising implications for sustainability.

Producing items closer to home means less distance for products to travel, fewer resources used for packaging, and less need for storage. It would also allow for a more on-demand production model, where items are created only when needed, reducing waste from overproduction. 3D printing technology makes it possible to create optimized designs that use fewer materials without sacrificing product quality. This efficiency could lead to less waste in the production process and less pressure on raw material sources. Additive manufacturing and 3D printing promote economic and social sustainability, too. These technologies could open doors for collaboration with people in disadvantaged countries. Empowered by digital technology, individuals could significantly use additive manufacturing to improve their economic position - for example, by managing the digital design of parts - and contribute to a more equitable global economy.

Personalization reduces waste

To some theorists, personalization could lead to increased consumption, as customized products become ever more appealing, causing individuals to buy more. The opposing school of thought, however, proposes that personalization could reduce material waste as people get exactly what they need with each purchase, resulting in fewer unwanted or discarded items. I am firmly in the latter camp. Let me explain why.

Two years ago, I experienced a physical condition that caused discomfort in my knees, particularly during colder seasons like winter and autumn. I realized that I needed 'longer' short running pants that could reach my knees to keep me warm when I go running. However, finding short pants to fit my specific needs was a struggle. I ended up spending €300 on a variety of products from Amazon and AliExpress, only to discover that most of them were not right. This experience illustrates the broader issue of waste generated due to the lack of personalization in product manufacturing. If I had the option to input my exact measurements on a website to receive a product tailored to my needs, not only would it have saved me money, but it would also have reduced the material waste generated from the numerous unsuitable products I purchased.

Personalization in this context goes beyond just a preference for our favorite colors; it addresses the individual physical conditions each of us has. In essence, it recognizes that we are not perfect; we each have unique needs and attributes. If personalization options were available, I would have been content buying just the right pair I needed, even at a slightly higher price, instead of wasting 300 Euros on nearly eighty pairs that I cannot use.

Therefore, as to whether a Post-Digital Society has the potential to be less wasteful, I believe the answer is yes. Hyper-personalization can help us meet individual needs more accurately, which in turn can reduce waste. It allows for products to be created that suit each person's unique physical attributes, breaking away from the "one size fits all" approach that is both environmentally harmful and often unsatisfactory for the consumer.

Ultimately, this move towards personalization empowers people, allowing them to dictate their needs rather than being subject to mass-produced trends. Digital technologies such as AI and machine learning could further be used to predict consumer needs and more accurately reduce overproduction and waste. 3D printing, which we discussed earlier, can be a powerful tool for personalization while reducing waste. By creating items on demand based on specific user specifications, 3D printing can minimize waste from unsold products and ensure that resources are used to develop genuinely desired and needed things.

Personalization could also lead to greater product satisfaction and longevity. If an item is tailored to users' needs and preferences, they may value it more and keep it longer. As always, we must consider the entire lifecycle of these personalized products-the source of their materials, the energy used to make them, and their disposal or recycling at the end of their useful life.

The Circular Economy realized

The so called 'Circular Economy' has long been talked about in environmental and business circles but remains elusive – always seemingly five years around the corner. Ironically, we have been going round in circles trying to achieve it.

In the words of the European Parliament, "The circular economy is a model of production and consumption, which involves sharing, leasing, reusing, repairing, refurbishing, and recycling existing materials and products as long as possible. In this way, the life cycle of products is extended. In practice, it implies reducing waste to a minimum." The multiple benefits of reusing and recycling products include slow downing the use of natural resources, reducing landscape and habitat disruption, helping to limit biodiversity loss and an overall a reduction in total annual greenhouse gas emissions. According to the European Environment Agency, industrial processes and product use are responsible for 9.1% of greenhouse gas emissions in the

EU, while the management of waste accounts for 3.32%.[88]

The Ellen MacArthur Foundation has been banging this drum since it was founded in 2010 – well over a decade ago – to promote circular economy practices. Its first economic report, delivered at Davos in 2012, stated:

> "The circular economy largely replaces the concept of a consumer with that of a user. This calls for a new contract between businesses and their customers based on product performance. Unlike in today's 'buy-and-consume' economy, durable products are leased, rented, or shared wherever possible. If they are sold, there are incentives or agreements in place to ensure the return and thereafter the reuse of the product or its components and materials at the end of its period of primary use."[89]

Does that passage remind you of anything? Yes, the now infamous WEF phrase: "you'll own nothing, and you'll be happy"! The circular economy gives us the means to make that a (positive!) reality.

The Post-Digital Society will finally see a circular economy emerge in reality, not just within the pages of reports. Through conversational and generative AI, we can better identify individual needs and create products from materials that are more easily recyclable, thus fostering circular practices. For instance, we can develop a product that can be recycled more effectively – perhaps even ground down into 3D printing pellets that can be reused again and again.

There are multiple case studies which give good reason for optimism. Plastic Bank for example empowers social recycling, cleaning up ocean plastic and helping to alleviate poverty for coastal communities. Its 'ethical collection communities' exchange ocean-bound plastic for income and life-improving benefits. Collected material is then processed into Social Plastic® feedstock for reuse in products and packaging. In doing so, it enables community members in vulnerable coastal areas to become recycling entrepreneurs, with the potential to lift millions out of poverty. As of 2022, it was operating in Indonesia, the Philippines, Egypt, and Brazil, with licensed partner-based expansion in Cameroon. Every transaction is "secured through an energy-efficient hybrid blockchain-secured platform that enables traceable collection, secure income, and real-time impact reporting."[90] Every exchange goes through the Plastic Bank app, offering a fully traceable recycling process which includes rewards and benefits and plastic credits (see tokenization), supply chain management, partner impact reporting, secure savings and income for collection community members. For the full year 2022, the Plastic Bank recovered almost 30m kilos of plastic pollution across 53 Certified Processor Partners and 817 collection branches. It also paid out over $2m in bonuses to its 21,791 active waste collectors.

Other examples include Ecosia: the search engine that uses its profits to plant trees worldwide, demonstrating how digital businesses can directly contribute to environmental sustainability. Or Fairphone: a Netherlands-based company that produces ethically sourced and manufactured smartphones. They focus on longevity and repairability, encouraging consumers to keep their phones longer, thereby reducing e-waste – while the raw materials used to create the phones are transparently sourced and fairly traded becoming, in essence, a 'fair trade' phone.

I am an entrepreneur and a capitalist, not a socialist. However, my approach to capitalism encompasses a deeper sense of responsibility and purpose beyond just financial gains. This perspective allows for a form of capitalism that considers the interests of all stakeholders, not just shareholders, promoting a more holistic and sustainable approach to business. In this regard, stakeholder capitalism aligns very well with the principles of a circular economy. It acknowledges that the planet is a significant stakeholder, along with others including shareholders, customers, suppliers, employees, and the wider environment. By adopting this broader viewpoint, we can foster a system that benefits not just those who are financially invested, but also other groups and the planet as a whole.

The token economy for example becomes a powerful

tool for incentivizing green and circular practices. The blockchain technology that underpins the token economy can create transparent and tamper-proof records, as seen in the Plastic Bank. This characteristic can be used to track and reward wider sustainable behavior in various ways. For example, tokens could be issued to reward individuals or businesses that engage in sustainable behaviors, such as recycling, reducing energy consumption, or participating in environmental conservation efforts. This system can promote a circular economy in which people are incentivized to make environmentally friendly choices. Tokens could also represent carbon credits in a blockchain-based market, making buying and selling carbon offsets more transparent and efficient. This could encourage companies to reduce carbon emissions, knowing their efforts can be accurately tracked and rewarded.

Sustainable by design

I have recently collaborated with Panasonic, the prominent multinational company that produces a wide range of products. During my collaboration with them, I have been privy to many internal strategies and rules they implement to foster green production processes and ensure that the products are designed to consume less energy. The sustainable design of technology is a focus, with an emphasis on creating products that are sustainable right from the design phase.

This "sustainable by design" approach means that products are developed with materials that can be recycled and circulated within the economy while consuming less energy than present products and performing the same functions. Moreover, they aim to have a lesser environmental impact during the production of these products. It transcends corporate self-responsibility, paving the way for more sustainable practices in the industry.

The idea of "sustainable by design" is becoming influential across multiple sectors. Cefic, the European Chemical Industry Council, for example, state: "We believe that criteria for chemicals that are safe and sustainable-by-design must address the three pillars of sustainability – environmental, social and economic factors – and take a life cycle approach." The European Commission has introduced the Ecodesign for Sustainable Products Regulation (ESPR), as part of the broader Sustainable Product Initiative, which provides a framework of legal requirements to improve the environmental sustainability of products. If managed carefully, sector innovation and progressive legislation can complement each other. As Cefic continues, the ESPR framework "is essential to the success of the Chemicals Strategy for Sustainability and can accelerate innovation in the chemical sector and the value chains we serve to the benefit of realizing the SDGs in general and the circularity and climate-neutrality objectives in particular."[91]

Meanwhile in the construction sector, research by engineering consultancy Patrick Parsons identified significant commercial benefits from using sustainable design and engineering to build developments with lower carbon footprint and water use, reduce waste and materials used. Eighty-three percent of respondents surveyed said that projects designed with green credentials have given them a competitive advantage while two thirds (66%) claim sustainable design is adding value to current developments, with 58% of respondents saying sustainable design will become even more important over the next three years.[92]

I was struck when reading a Panasonic survey of over a thousand business professionals in Germany and the United Kingdom, which gauged their awareness of sustainability measures and corporate priorities, by how often opinions were focused on two priorities, namely:

- **Reducing emissions of its own value chain (Scope 1, 2 and 3).**

- **Avoiding CO2 emissions through existing and new technologies and businesses.**

If we were to view each of these commitments as one instead of separately, then the logical conclusion would be that by doing both, we can do much more. If each company — in addition to reducing emissions that are tied to its value chain — should evaluate how its business purpose can add value with regard to avoiding emissions, then it can help others to become more sustainable and reduce the amount of energy they consume during everyday activities and tasks. Transforming the operating model of a major corporation is no small feat. However, with the right strategy, vision, and investments, it can become far more feasible. It's worth emphasizing that, in the same study, 80% of the interviewees claimed that "environmental sustainability plays an important role in purchase decisions and the procurement process." In other words, there is a growing trend towards value investing, which makes 'sustainable by design' a no-brainer.

Forging the right path

The digital technology needed to drive the Post-Digital Society will undoubtedly consume significant energy. Data centers, which underpin the Internet and the vast cloud services we already use daily, are major electricity consumers and contribute significantly to global carbon emissions – our need for data centers will only increase exponentially with AI, IoT and autonomous vehicles. However, the emissions don't come from the power needs of the sectors, *per se*, but rather how that electricity is produced. As we rapidly adopt green, clean, renewable energy, so the emissions related to data centers (to stay with that example) decrease potentially to zero.

According to The International Renewable Energy Agency (IRENA), in 2022, of the 60 countries with targets for renewable defined as a share of the power mix, 14 committed to achieving less than 24% share of renewable energy, 22 committed to shares between 25% and 59%, 13 committed to shares between 60% and 89%, while 11 Parties committed to shares between 90% to 100%. And far from the fear that developing nations will want to develop along fossil fuel lines, most of the countries that have committed to 100% renewables in their electricity mix by 2030 are small island developing states. The energy transition is happening, therefore, and our electricity production is becoming ever greener and cleaner.

The role of renewable energy in the energy transition

93

2018

378EJ Total Final Energy Consumption

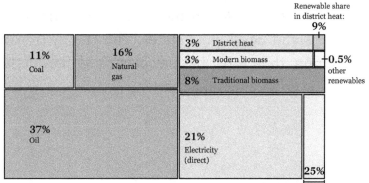

2050

Where we need to be (1.5-S)

348EJ Total Final Energy Consumption

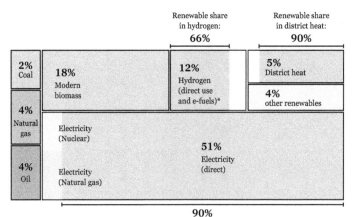

Source: IRENA

Cryptocurrency is a case in point. Whether cryptocurrencies will become less carbon-intensive than physical cash is complex and largely depends on the evolution of the technology behind these digital currencies. Many cryptocurrencies, such as Bitcoin, are known for their high energy consumption. This is due to the computationally intensive process known as "mining," which is required to verify and add transactions to the blockchain. However, not all cryptocurrencies use the same mechanisms. For example, newer cryptocurrencies implement more energy-efficient protocols, potentially reducing their carbon footprint. Again, ultimately the carbon intensity of cryptocurrencies depends mainly on the type of energy used. If cryptocurrency's electricity comes from renewable sources, the carbon footprint would be significantly lower than if it came from fossil fuels. It's also important to note that the current production and distribution of physical cash currency also has environmental costs, including the resources used to mint coins or print notes and the energy used to transport cash. In the long run, cryptocurrencies in a Post-Digital Society can evolve to use less energy-intensive processes and draw their power from renewable sources, becoming far less carbon-intensive than physical cash.

Indeed, the transition to a Post-Digital Society holds the potential for a 'post-carbon' world. Many countries and companies have set targets for net-zero carbon emissions between 2030 and 2050. Advances in technology could further facilitate the transition to a net-zero carbon world, with digital tools and systems that help streamline and optimize transportation, production, and consumption processes. AI can also provide the means to closely monitor and effectively manage our environmental impact, providing the critical data we need to make more informed and sustainable decisions. For example, Contrails from airplanes are condensation trails that trap heat in the atmosphere and are responsible for more than a third of aviation's global warming impact, according to the 2022 Intergovernmental Panel on Climate Change (IPCC) Report. An AI experiment in 2023, led by Google Research, American Airlines and Bill Gates's Breakthrough Energy, identified routes that avoided the atmospheric conditions that create Contrails. In a series of test flights, pilots were able to reduce contrails by an astonishing 54 per cent[94]. Given such a significant success rate, it's not hard to imagine what could be achieved if we turned powerful AI to other sustainability and emissions issues.

But while technology can and should play a critical role in this transition, it's important to remember that achieving a post-carbon world will require significant systemic and societal changes. These include changes in policy, business practices, societal attitudes, and individual behavior. The transition to net zero is not a purely technological challenge but a socio-economic and political one.

A critical point of optimism, however, is that the foundation of a Post-Digital Society lies in empowering individuals. This approach can make a significant difference by allowing people to be directly involved in sustainability decisions. My hope is that this ground-up approach can achieve what current leaders, often tangled in hegemonic and bureaucratic hurdles, struggle to reach. Empowering individuals with knowledge, tools, and a voice can drive significant change. In the post-digital world, where people can contribute, collaborate, and innovate across traditional boundaries, we can foster a collective commitment to sustainability. In doing so, we can move the vision of a post-carbon society from aspiration to reality.

Dodging the Digital Divide

One of the critical social sustainability challenges I foresee is the "digital divide." Despite the rapid spread of digital technologies, access is still not universal. Millions of people worldwide, particularly in rural areas and developing countries, lack reliable Internet access, which can marginalize those individuals and communities socially, economically, and politically. The digital divide also extends to digital literacy, as some people within developed countries too lack the skills to navigate the digital world effectively.

As we move into a post-digital age, there remains a significant gap in access to and understanding technology. Bridging this gap means empowering more people to participate in sustainable practices and benefit from the efficiencies that technology can bring. As we move forward, it's vital to ensure that digital resources are available and accessible to all, and that people are educated on how to use them.

I believe it's critical, particularly for societies to address and actively work towards bridging the digital divide. This divide is apparent not just globally, but within our societies as well, affecting different age groups (albeit it is anticipated that the age-related digital divide will gradually diminish as newer generations are naturally more adept with digital technology). This initiative shouldn't just be the responsibility of the governments, but also of companies and the general populace.

Addressing the digital divide isn't just about providing access to digital resources; it also encompasses fostering digital literacy and education. As leaders in the global community, it's incumbent upon us to assume a positive leadership role. This leadership should encourage development and prevent exploitation of resources in developing countries. Once the infrastructure is in place, it paves the way for economic development, and we can actively participate to assist communities in adapting to the digital age. For instance, if we consider the situation in Niger, Africa, it appears that the primary interest has been in harnessing its uranium resources, rather than fostering sustainable development in the region. This approach, exploiting natural resources without building necessary infrastructure or considering the welfare of the local community, is unacceptable. To effect positive change, it is vital to engage in constructive efforts that involve investment and building essential structures.

However, efforts must also be concentrated on eradicating corruption that can be pervasive at both the corporate and governmental levels in various societies, not just in the West. To truly make a difference, Western societies need to embody positive leadership by leading through example. This approach will hopefully steer us in the right direction and create a more inclusive and equitable digital future for everyone. It might seem like a Herculean task, and might need adjustments along the way, but it is necessary to foster a world where resources and opportunities are accessible to all.

This vision of a sustainable Post-Digital Society should be more than an aspiration – it must be our shared commitment, a global pledge to use technology to enhance, not diminish, all our lives. The power of the Post-Digital Society lies not in the hands of the technology itself but in the people who use it. We are the guardians of this digital dawn and have a collective responsibility to steer its course toward sustainable and equitable shores.

Our journey into the post-digital age can be an epic voyage toward social, economic, and environmental sustainability. The challenges are immense, but so are the opportunities. We must use technology as an enabler, a catalyst that empowers people and drives social progress while supporting a more resilient and sustainable economy. But we must never forget that technology is only a tool - our choices and actions will shape its impact. As such, we have a critical role in shaping a future where no one is left behind.

CONCLUSION

Deciding our future

In the Introduction, we visualized crossing the bridge toward our post-digital future. Since the beginning of the Digital Transformation journey, there has been continuous progress, but the bridge is still under construction. To have the courage to complete it and make the crossing, we must take heart from our shared history. Time and again, we have risen to meet the challenges of our time. From our collective human experience, cooperative action has been the bedrock of societal progress since immemorial. We have consistently demonstrated our ability to adapt, innovate, and expand the realm of possibility in the face of daunting challenges. The transition to a sustainable, peaceful Post-Digital Society is another such shared endeavor that we can meet and overcome as a global community.

As we embark on this journey together, the importance of unity cannot be overstated. The power of collaboration is a beacon that guides us through obstacles and promotes positive change. Using technology as a tool for progress rather than a passive bystander, and our active engagement with technology for our own betterment, is a shared responsibility that falls on all of us.

At the time of writing this, amid the current geopolitical

landscape is a significant tension surrounding cryptocurrencies, especially in the US. The US is apprehensive about
losing power and influence if the US dollar loses its position as the global reserve currency. This, in turn, affects
cryptocurrencies and the decentralized autonomous organizations (DAOs) globally, including countries that have
close ties with the US, like Germany, the UK, and other
European nations.

Simultaneously, BRICS nations are considering adopting
a common digital currency, representing a departure from
traditional approaches, and possibly indicating a shift
towards a new multilateral world order. As reported by
Reuters in August 2023, Luiz Inacio Lula da Silva made the
following proposal at a BRICS summit in Johannesburg:
"Brazil's president doesn't believe nations that don't use
the dollar should be forced to trade in the currency, and he
has also advocated for a common currency in the Merco-
sur bloc of South American countries. A BRICS currency
'increases our payment options and reduces our vulnera-
bilities," he told the summit's opening plenary session."[95]
Whether this happens or not, the significance of the proposal being a cryptocurrency should not be underestimated. As cryptocurrency analyst Bhushan Akolkar blogged:

> "...adoption by BRICS countries can facilita-
> te trade and financial transactions within the
> group and with other nations outside the con-
> ventional banking system. This becomes parti-

cularly significant for developing economies within BRICS, where a significant portion of the
population remains unbanked or underbanked,
enabling greater financial inclusion. Countries
like China, Brazil, and India are already exploring the possibility of having a central bank digital currency (CBDC) in their regions. As per
the latest reports, the central bank of Brazil joined hands with giants like Microsoft and VISA
for the CBDC pilot."[96]

Again, whether the CBDC itself succeeds is a moot point.
But the direction of travel – and its logical anti-hegemo-
nic reasoning – is clear. Moving forward, the focus will be
on decentralizing power and promoting financial systems
that prioritize the welfare of the populace over centralized
power structures. This vision calls for a re-evaluation and
potential overhaul of existing financial frameworks, fostering a future where power is evenly distributed and a global
economy that is driven by the collective decision-making
of the people. If we are witnessing a growing consensus on
the need to develop a new exchange currency that is uni-
versally backed and offers flexibility, then digital currencies, particularly cryptocurrencies, are the most (or only)
viable route to achieve this.

To zoom out and take a macro-historical perspective, this
evolution been underway for centuries. From monarchies
to parliamentary democracies to universal suffrage, the

progression has always been towards amplifying people's voices and power. In the Post-Digital Society, technology will further facilitate this empowerment, potentially unsettling existing power dynamics.

I interact with European politicians regularly due to my collaboration with the European Commission, and sometimes, I perceive a genuine concern among many regarding these shifting trends powered by digital technology. These shifts point towards a trajectory whereby power returns to the people, cutting out the delegates and breaking away from the elitist structures that have historically held sway.

The emphasis should now be on recognizing the potential for a more democratized, people-centric future where the influence of the establishment diminishes. I have said that in the Post-Digital Society we will "take the stage as actors, not as mere spectators". We will have more control, more autonomy, not less – this is a very positive future, yet one that hasn't been widely communicated yet. We must all do our utmost to share this vision.

The Triumvirate: Blockchain, Web3, and the Metaverse

At the dawn of the Post-Digital Society, as we step off the bridge at the other side, we will see a world where blockchain, Web 3.0, and the Metaverse form a mighty triumvirate. Much like Caesar's political structures of ancient Rome, this triumvirate sees each reinforcing the others, creating a formidable force – this time, shaping the contours of our evolving digital landscape. Blockchain, with its promise of decentralized and secure transactions; Web 3.0, championing a user-centric and intelligent Internet; and the Metaverse, offering infinite virtual spaces for interaction and innovation — these are no longer the shiny novelties of an earlier era. They are becoming as integral to our lives as running water, electricity, or the telephone. In our emerging Post-Digital Society, much like we take utilities for granted, we are growing accustomed to the digital tools that once seemed so revolutionary. As they become the norm, they are redefining how we interact, transact, and democratize our societies.

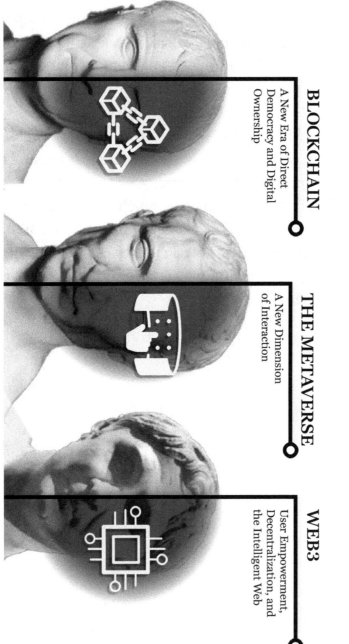

The Triumvirate of the Post-Digital Society

BLOCKCHAIN
A New Era of Direct Democracy and Digital Ownership

THE METAVERSE
A New Dimension of Interaction

WEB3
User Empowerment, Decentralization, and the Intelligent Web

Infographic by Antonio Grasso

The Triumvirate of blockchain, Web 3.0, and the Metaverse is not just a set of tools, but a catalyst for a significant societal transformation. As we have seen throughout this book, blockchain, the first pillar of this triad, is more than just the technology behind cryptocurrencies like Bitcoin. It's a digital, decentralized, and immutable ledger that allows for the transfer of any digital asset with security and transparency without intermediary entities. This principle of disintermediation is one of its most transformative aspects. It removes the need for central authorities, such as banks or governments, in transactions. In doing so, it places individuals at the heart of economic and democratic dynamics, empowering them in previously unimaginable ways. The concept of direct democracy, where citizens have a direct and unmediated influence over policy decisions, becomes feasible with blockchain. The immutability of blockchain, which ensures that once data is entered it cannot be tampered with, provides the security and trust needed to implement direct democracy. The implications of this will be resisted by the establishment and other intermediaries impacted for as long as they can hold out, but they will – I believe – eventually be undeniable.

Decentralized Autonomous Organizations (DAOs) too are a powerful realization of blockchain's potential. Governed by rules encoded as smart contracts on the blockchain, these organizations embody the principle of disintermediation, removing traditional management hierarchies and placing power in the hands of individual participants. The 'code is law' ethos underpinning DAOs aligns with blockchain's immutability, as the rules defined in smart contracts cannot be changed without consensus. This approach eliminates bureaucracy, fosters efficiency, and supports the 'code is law' philosophy, where encoded rules replace traditional governance structures.

The second pillar, Web 3.0, represents the evolution of the Internet into a decentralized, intelligent, user-centric platform. The control and ownership of data and services are distributed across the network rather than being held by a central authority like a big tech company. This shift in architecture allows for increased privacy, security, and user control. Unlike the earlier versions of the web, Web 3.0 is built on the idea that users should have control over their data. This shift fundamentally changes the relationship between users and online platforms, allowing individuals to maintain their privacy while benefiting from personalized experiences. In a Web 3.0 environment, data is not locked away in siloed databases but is accessible to the user who generated it. This democratization of data control can have profound implications for how we use the Internet, towards a more service-oriented architecture, where applications can utilize user-controlled data from various sources to provide tailored services. This will see a shift to token-based economics (tokenomics), used to incentivize and reward user participation, create new business models, or even function as a network exchange medium. Tokenization opens up new possibilities for economic interaction, including direct peer-to-peer transactions, without a centralized intermediary. As the amount of data continues to grow, AI and machine learning algorithms are needed to make sense of it all. They can analyze and learn from large volumes of data to provide more accurate search results, better recommendations, and more personalized user experiences. But perhaps more importantly, AI can enable the automation of tasks and services, paving the way for a more interactive, autonomous, and dynamic web.

The third pillar of this triad, the Metaverse, is often visualized as a virtual reality space where users can interact with a computer-generated environment and other users. However, as we saw in Chapter Five, the Metaverse is more than just an advanced user interface; it is a convergence of virtual reality (VR), augmented reality (AR), AI, and the Internet, with blockchain and Web 3.0 forming its backbone. The myth of Romulus becoming Quirinus, transcending physicality, becomes real within the Metaverse. It speaks to a human desire to transcend the earthly plane and become something greater, be it a god or a digital entity unfettered by physical limitations. In the Metaverse we can adopt new identities and roles that surpass our physical selves. The figure of Quirinus also represented the unity and protection of the Roman people. In the Metaverse, the interconnected nature of the virtual world fosters a new kind of communal unity, where traditional barriers of language, geography, and culture dissolve.

Connecting through headsets to the Metaverse will soon be as commonplace as logging on to the internet today. There are endless possibilities in this new realm, quite distinct from our current way of life. The boundary between the physical and digital realms is already blurring, and we need to adapt to this transformation. We continue to enjoy physical experiences such as dining out, going on vacations, and meeting friends. Yet, we are also realizing that we can engage in these activities in new ways within the digital sphere. Of course, these two experiences are different, but the Metaverse offers novel methods to do things we already enjoy. For instance, I might be able to visit a concert in Japan, something I couldn't do physically from Naples. Through the Metaverse, I can virtually travel and immerse myself in a multitude of experiences, bridging the physical and digital worlds in a seamless loop that enhances our society and personal lives.

Moreover, the growth of the Metaverse could potentially foster a more sustainable lifestyle. By reducing the necessity for travel, we could lessen our carbon footprint and revitalize local communities. This new focus on local living could result in greener urban centers and bolster local economies, creating a more sustainable future. For example, in the Metaverse we may increasingly 'shop' for digital things, not physical things, thus reducing our material consumption; our physical needs sought and met more locally than now. The emergence of the Metaverse offers intriguing possibilities for sustainability. Our need to travel will also reduce, potentially flying and driving less, reducing travel emissions. The shift toward purchasing digital rather than physical goods could significantly reduce material consumption. This, in turn, could lessen the strain on our natural resources and reduce waste. In addition, immersive virtual experiences could replace some of our need for physical travel, lowering emissions, mainly from air travel. The servers and infrastructure that power digital spaces like the Metaverse will consume significant amounts of energy. That's why an energy transition must complement our digital transformation. Our efforts to reduce material consumption and carbon emissions must be matched by strategies to improve energy efficiency and increase the use of renewable energy sources.

Indeed, this progression toward a Post-Digital Society may naturally lead to a post-carbon society – as we saw in the final chapter. This shift is fueled by an increased awareness of climate change and the impacts of our actions on the environment. As we embrace a Post-Digital Society, it is imperative to also prioritize the wellbeing of our planet. After all, while the Earth has the capacity to heal itself over time, humanity faces a more immediate threat.

The post-carbon society and the Post-Digital Society are therefore united. This is a hopeful vision, far removed from the scaremongering of robots taking our jobs, of catastrophic climate change, or the 'singularity'. I don't mean to patronize or discount those concepts or potential futures – they are all valid and indeed possible. But the future I paint in this book, the Post-Digital Society, is, I believe, far more likely, far more positive, and yet – strangely – much less discussed.

The vision of a sustainable Post-Digital Society should be more than an aspiration – it must be our shared commitment. It is a global pledge to utilize technology to enhance, not diminish, the quality of our lives. The power of the Post-Digital Society lies not solely in the hands of technology but within the actions of the people who use it. We are the stewards of this digital dawn, responsible for guiding its course towards sustainable and equitable futures. Our venture into the post-digital age has the potential to be an epic journey toward social, economic, and environmental sustainability. The challenges we face should not be underestimated; but neither should the opportunities. We must leverage technology as an enabler, a catalyst that empowers individuals, drives social progress, and supports a more resilient and sustainable economy.

Throughout our collective human experience, cooperative action has consistently been the bedrock of societal progress. We have repeatedly demonstrated our ability to adapt, innovate, and expand the realm of possibility in the face of significant challenges. The emergence of a sustainable Post-Digital Society is merely the latest in this continuum of collective endeavors.

As we embark on this journey, the significance of unity and

collaboration comes to the fore. The power of cooperation serves as a guiding light, illuminating our path through obstacles and fostering positive change. Engaging actively with technology, using it as a tool for progress rather than a passive bystander, is a shared responsibility. Let's harness this collective strength to shape our digital future, striving to build a world that improves our lives and planet.

As we discussed regarding the BRICS nations, they don't have to follow the development path of so-called 'Western' countries. They have the opportunity to directly adopt renewable energy sources and integrate cryptocurrencies if they choose to. While we cannot ignore the current tensions between China and the USA, which have brought us closer to potential global conflict (as indicated by the "Doomsday Clock" standing at just 90 seconds to midnight[97]), assuming we can avoid a third world war, I project that by 2035 we will be living in the Post-Digital Society. It will be a natural progression – one that we may not even notice unfolding. By 2035 and heading into the 2040s, we will have entered a new reality, a world centered around sharing more than just bits and bytes for entertainment but sharing ourselves, our values, and our knowledge to benefit others.

I envision a world where power is more evenly distributed among the many rather than being concentrated in the hands of a few. Where finance has broken from the shackles of centralization. Where business is run by employees and stakeholders, not bosses and shareholders. Where one-size-fits-all wasteful consumerism is replaced by personalization and the circular economy. A low waste, low-carbon world. A world where the creativity of individuals is recognized and rewarded, supported by machines, not replaced by them. A world where man and machine, AI and the environment, integrate seamlessly together. I sincerely hope that we can work together to achieve this world. With our collective leadership, we can realize this better future.

REFERENCES

INTRODUCTION

1   Chris Miller, 'Chip War: The Fight for the World's Most Critical Technology', Simon and Schuster, 2022

2   Ping, G. 'Digital Transformation – Maslow's Hierarchy of Needs'. Huawei Tech, Nov 2017. https://www.huawei.com/en/huaweitech/industry-insights/outlook/asia-pacific-innovation-day-2017-guoping

3   European Commission. '2050 long-term strategy'. https://climate.ec.europa.eu/eu-action/climate-strategies-targets/2050-long-term-strategy_en

CHAPTER ONE

4   World Economic Forum. '8 predictions for the world in 2030'. Facebook. 18 Nov 2016. https://www.facebook.com/worldeconomicforum/videos/10153920524981479/

5   McCall, I. 'World Economic Forum: 8 Deadly Predictions for 2030 – Great Reset'. Medium. 10 June 2022. https://medium.com/yardcouch-com/world-economic-forum-8-deadly-predictions-for-2030-great-reset-3f799b7afe9c (Accessed: date).

6   Taki. 'Is Klaus Schwab the greatest threat of our time?'. The Spectator. 14 May 2022 https://www.spectator.co.uk/article/is-klaus-schwab-the-greatest-threat-of-our-time/

7   Auken, Ida. 'Welcome To 2030: I Own Nothing, Have No Privacy And Life Has Never Been Better', Forbes. 2016, November 10. Retrieved from https://www.forbes.com/sites/worldeconomicforum/2016/11/10/shopping-i-cant-really-remember-what-that-is-or-how-differently-well-live-in-2030/

8   Statista. (no date). 'Quarterly number of Netflix streaming subscribers worldwide'. Available at: https://www.statista.com/statistics/250934/quarterly-number-of-netflix-streaming-subscribers-worldwide/ (Accessed: date).
Statista. (no date). 'Number of paying Spotify subscribers'. Available at: https://www.statista.com/statistics/244995/number-of-paying-spotify-subscribers/ (Accessed: date).

9   Kevin Kelly. "The Inevitable: Understanding the 12 Technological Forces That Will Shape Our Future

10   D'Antonio, M., Gerzema, J. (2010). Spend Shift: How the Post-Crisis Values Revolution Is Changing the Way We Buy, Sell, and Live. Germany: Wiley.

11   Toffler, Alvin. The Third Wave. Bantam Books, 1980.

12   Benkler, Yochai. The Wealth of Networks: How Social Production Transforms Markets and Freedom. Yale University Press, 2006.

13   Jin, L. (2020, October 6). The Creator Economy Needs a Middle Class. Harvard Business Review.

14   Drenik, G. (2022, August 23). The Creator Economy Is Booming: Here's How Businesses Can Tap Into Its Potential. Forbes. Retrieved from https://www.forbes.com/sites/garydrenik/2022/08/23/the-creator-economy-is-booming-heres-how-businesses-can-tap-into-its-potential/?sh=2084f1ed3d27

15   New Scientist. (n.d.). Anne-Marie Imafidon: AI and the Future of Work [Video]. Retrieved from https://www.newscientist.com/video/2184176-anne-marie-imafidon-ai-and-the-future-of-work/

16   Petrescu, R. V., & Avasilcai, S. (2018). A perspective on the potential of blockchain technology for the EU: A mechanism for trust and transparency. European Journal of Law and Technology, 9(1), 1-12. doi: 10.1007/s10978-018-9226-y

17   The Parliament Magazine. (n.d.). EU must work to enable blockchain technology. Retrieved from https://www.theparliamentmagazine.eu/news/article/eu-must-work-to-enable-blockchain-technology. Accessed 05 April 2023.

18   Tapscott, D. (2016). Blockchain revolution: how the technology behind bitcoin is changing money, business, and the world. Penguin.

CHAPTER TWO

19   Carne, R. (2017). The Accidental Anarchist. TEDxSkoll. https://www.youtube.com/watch?v=2Hc2_jY4KhY&ab_channel=TEDxTalks

20   Gorbis, M. (2013). The nature of the future: Dispatches from the

socialstructed world. Free Press.

21   World Economic Forum. (2019, December 30). Why we need the Davos manifesto for a better kind of capitalism. https://www.weforum.org/agenda/2019/12/why-we-need-the-davos-manifesto-for-better-kind-of-capitalism/

22   Business Roundtable. (2019, August 19). Business Roundtable redefines the purpose of a corporation to promote 'An Economy That Serves All Americans.' https://www.businessroundtable.org/business-roundtable-redefines-the-purpose-of-a-corporation-to-promote-an-economy-that-serves-all-americans

23   https://www.weforum.org/agenda/2019/12/why-we-need-the-davos-manifesto-for-better-kind-of-capitalism/

24   Marker. (2020, March 24). It's time for CEOs to emerge from their bunkers. https://marker.medium.com/its-time-for-ceos-to-emerge-from-their-bunkers-b696cfdc678e

25   Brixton Pound. (n.d.). About the Brixton Pound. https://brixtonpound.org/

26   Algorand Foundation. (2021, March 30). Brixton Pound and Algorand. https://www.algorand.foundation/news/brixton-pound-algorand

27   Zuckerberg, M. (2019, March 29). Mark Zuckerberg: The internet needs new rules. Let's start in these four areas. The Washington Post. https://www.washingtonpost.com/opinions/mark-zuckerberg-the-internet-needs-new-rules-lets-start-in-these-four-areas/2019/03/29/9e6f0504-521a-11e9-a3f7-78b7525a8d5f_story.html

28   Pasquale, F. (2015). The black box society: The secret algorithms that control money and information. Harvard University Press.

29   https://www.rand.org/content/dam/rand/pubs/research_reports/RR1700/RR1744/RAND_RR1744.pdf

30   https://www.cbsnews.com/news/pope-francis-puffer-jacket-fake-photos-deepfake-power-peril-of-ai

31   Liu, A. (2018). The future of work in the globalized digital age: A strategic guide. United Nations Department of Economic and Social Affairs. https://www.un.org/esa/desa/papers/2018/wp156_2018.pdf

32   Rodrik, D. (2011). The globalization paradox: Democracy and the future of the world economy. W. W. Norton & Company.

33   World Economic Forum. (2018, November 13). Globalization 4.0: What does it mean, how it will benefit everyone. https://www.weforum.org/agenda/2018/11/globalization-4-what-does-it-mean-how-it-will-benefit-everyone/

34   Guttentag, D. A., & Park, S. Y. (2022). Metaverse beyond the hype: Multidisciplinary perspectives on emerging challenges, opportunities, and agenda for research, practice and policy. International Journal of Information Management, 66, 102542. https://doi.org/10.1016/j.ijinfomgt.2022.102542

35   Ellard, A. (2023, March 29). DDG Ellard: The future of globalization is services, digital technology [Speech]. Georgetown University Global Trade Academy. https://www.wto.org/english/news_e/news23_e/ddgae_29mar23_e.htm

CHAPTER THREE

36   Patent: "US4131919A." Espacenet. Available at: https://worldwide.espacenet.com/patent/search/family/025174681/publication/US4131919A?q=pn%3DUS4131919.

37   Standing, Craig & Kiniti, Sarah. (2011). "How can organizations use wikis for innovation?" Technovation, 31, 287-295. doi: 10.1016/j.technovation.2011.02.005.

38   Website: "Works Council." Handbook Germany. Available at: https://handbookgermany.de/en/works-council.

39   Website: "It's Time for CEOs to Emerge from Their Bunkers." Marker. Available at: https://marker.medium.com/its-time-for-ceos-to-emerge-from-their-bunkers-b696cfdc678e.

40   Website: "Novo Nordisk." Shared Value Initiative. Available at: https://www.sharedvalue.org/partner/novo-nordisk/.

41   Website: "Novo Nordisk Revenue 2006-2021." MacroTrends. Available at: https://www.macrotrends.net/stocks/charts/NVO/novo-nordisk/revenue.

42   White Paper: "Measuring Stakeholder Capitalism Towards Common Metrics and Consistent Reporting of Sustainable Value Creation."

(September 2020). World Economic Forum. Available at:
https://www3.weforum.org/docs/WEF_IBC_Measuring_Stakeholder_
Capitalism_Report_2020.pdf.

43   Website: "BusyDAO White Paper." BusyDAO. Available at:
https://busydao.io/attachments/white-paper.pdf.

44   Article: Grieves, M. (2017). "Digital twin: Mitigating unpredictable,
undesirable emergent behavior in complex systems." The International
Journal of Aviation Psychology, 27(3-4), 146-152. doi:
10.1080/10508414.2017.1362430.

45   Website: "Repsol deploys its Production Management Digital Twin."
LinkedIn. Available at: https://www.linkedin.com/pulse/repsol-deploys-
its-production-management-digital-twin-guillermo/.

46   Website: "Digital Transformation in the Intelligent Enterprise." Accenture.
Available at: [https://www.accenture.com/us-en/blogs/technology-
innovation/daugherty-digital-transformation](https://www.ac

CHAPTER FOUR

47   Vaswani et al, Attention is All You Need, 2017.
https://arxiv.org/pdf/1706.03762.pdf

48   David Nield. "ChatGPT has passed the Turing test, and if you're freaked
out, you're not alone." TechRadar, Month Day, Year. Available at:
https://www.techradar.com/opinion/chatgpt-has-passed-the-turing-test-
and-if-youre-freaked-out-youre-not-alone.

49   Martineau, K. 'What is generative AI?' IBM Blog. 20 Apr 2023,
https://research.ibm.com/blog/what-is-generative-AI

50   McKinsey & Company. "What is generative AI?" McKinsey Explainers.
Available at: https://www.mckinsey.com/featured-insights/mckinsey-
explainers/what-is-generative-ai.

51   National Geographic Education. "Nanotechnology." Available at:
https://education.nationalgeographic.org/resource/nanotechnology/.

52   Medical Device Network. "Nanotechnology in medicine: How it could
shape the future of healthcare." Available at: https://www.medicaldevice-
network.com/comment/nanotechnology-medicine-technology/.

53   Carnegie Mellon University College of Engineering. "Yang and Cohen-
      Karni receive NSF award to study graphene-based neural probes.",
      Aug 2017, Available at: https://engineering.cmu.edu/news-events/
      news/2017/08/01-graphene-yang-cohen-karni.html.

54   The Digital Speaker. "The Materials Revolution: Nanotechnology and AI."
      Available at: https://www.thedigitalspeaker.com/materials-revolution-
      nanotechnology-ai/.

55   Pew Research Center. "The Metaverse in 2040.", June 2022. Available at:
      https://www.pewresearch.org/internet/2022/06/30/the-metaverse-
      in-2040/.

56   Andrew Makarow, "Augmented Reality Trends: What to Expect from
      Future AR Technologies." Mobidev, Aug 2022. Available at: https://
      mobidev.biz/blog/augmented-reality-trends-future-ar-technologies.

57   Pocket-lint. "Meta Project Cambria mixed reality headset: Release date,
      features, and news." Available at: https://www.pocket-lint.com/ar-vr/
      news/facebook/161118-meta-project-cambria-mixed-reality-headset-
      release-date-features/.

58   PEW RESEARCH CENTERJUNE 'The Metaverse in 2040', 30 June, 2022
      https://www.pewresearch.org/internet/2022/06/30/the-metaverse-
      in-2040/

59   Jaishy, S. (2023). "The Future of AIoT (AI+IoT)." LinkedIn. Available at:
      https://www.linkedin.com/pulse/future-ai-iot-aiot-shivashish-jaishy/.

60   Premio Inc. "AIoT and the Future of Industrial 4.0." 25 Augist, 202. Blog.
      Available at: https://premioinc.com/blogs/blog/aiot-and-the-future-of-
      industrial-4-0

61   World Economic Forum. (2023, March). "Trends for the Future of
      Cybersecurity." Available at: https://www.weforum.org/agenda/2023/03/
      trends-for-future-of-cybersecurity/

62   Bitdefender Business Insights. "How Quantum Computing Will Impact
      Cybersecurity." 13 October, 2021. Available at: https://www.bitdefender.
      co.uk/blog/businessinsights/how-quantum-computing-will-impact-
      cybersecurity/.

63   Microsoft Azure. (Year). "What is a qubit?" Available at: https://azure.
      microsoft.com/en-us/resources/cloud-computing-dictionary/

what-is-a-qubit/#introduction

64   New Statesman. (2022, November). "Cybersecurity in the Quantum Age."
     18 November, 2022. Available at: https://www.newstatesman.com/
     spotlight/cybersecurity/2022/11/cybersecurity-in-the-quantum-age

65   Nield, D. 'Fluxonium Qubit Retains Information For 1.43 Milliseconds'.
     Science Alert. O6 Jul, 2023. https://www.sciencealert.com/fluxonium-
     qubit-retains-information-for-1-43-milliseconds-10x-longer-than-before

66   KPMG. (2023, June). "Quantum Computers: The Emerging Cybersecurity
     Threat." Available at: https://kpmg.com/uk/en/blogs/home/posts/
     2023/06/quantum-computers-the-emerging-cybersecurity-threat.html

67   IBM News Room. (2022, November 9). "IBM Unveils 400-Qubit Plus
     Quantum Processor and Next-Generation IBM Quantum System Two."
     Available at: https://newsroom.ibm.com/2022-11-09-IBM-Unveils-400-
     Qubit-Plus-Quantum-Processor-and-Next-Generation-IBM-Quantum-
     System-Two

68   IBM News Room. (2022, November 9). "IBM Unveils 400-Qubit Plus
     Quantum Processor and Next-Generation IBM Quantum System Two."
     Available at: https://newsroom.ibm.com/2022-11-09-IBM-Unveils-400-
     Qubit-Plus-Quantum-Processor-and-Next-Generation-IBM-Quantum-
     System-Two

69   Premio Inc. "AIoT and the Future of Industrial 4.0." Premio Inc. Blog.
     25 Aug, 2021. Available at: https://premioinc.com/blogs/blog/aiot-and-
     the-future-of-industrial-4-0

70   Swabey, Pete. "Privacy on the Edge: Why Edge Computing Is a Double-
     Edged Sword for Privacy." Tech Monitor. 23 Feb, 2022. Available at:
     https://techmonitor.ai/focus/privacy-on-the-edge-why-edge-computing-
     is-a-double-edged-sword-for-privacy

CHAPTER FIVE

71   Plutarch, "The Life of Romulus".

72   World Economic Forum (2022) 'How web3 will transform the Internet',
     Available at: https://www.weforum.org/agenda/2022/02/web3-
     transform-the-internet/

73   Ibid

74   Fujitsu Global (2023) 'Blog Post', Available at: https://corporate-blog.
global.fujitsu.com/fgb/2023-01-11/01/

75   Sandvine (n.d.) 'Netflix vs. Google vs. Amazon vs. Facebook vs.
Microsoft vs. Apple: Traffic Share of Internet Brands Global Internet
Phenomena Spotlight', Available at: https://www.sandvine.com/blog/
netflix-vs.-google-vs.-amazon-vs.-facebook-vs.-microsoft-

76   ConsenSys (n.d.) 'Decentralized Finance', Available at:
https://consensys.net/blockchain-use-cases/decentralized-finance/

77   The Conversation (n.d.) 'Web 3.0: The decentralised web promises
to make the Internet free again', Available at: https://theconversation.
com/web-3-0-the-decentralised-web-promises-to-make-the-internet-
free-again-113139

78   Kafka, P. (2023) 'Neal Stephenson created the meta-idea all the tech
giants are now racing to make a reality', Vox, Available at:
https://www.vox.com/technology/2023/3/6/23627351/neal-
stephenson-snow-crash-metaverse-goggles-movies-games-tv-podcast-
peter-kafka-media-column.

79   Blockchain Magazine (n.d.) 'Is There Only 1 Metaverse? Can There
Be More?', Available at: https://blockchainmagazine.net/is-there-only-
1-metaverse-can-there-be-more/

80   Clegg, N. (2022) 'Making the Metaverse: What It Is, How It Will Be
Built, and Why It Matters', Medium, Available at: https://nickclegg.
medium.com/making-the-metaverse-what-it-is-how-it-will-be-built-
and-why-it-matters-3710f7570b04

81   The Street (2023) 'Mark Zuckerberg Quietly Buries the Metaverse',
Available at: https://www.thestreet.com/technology/mark-zuckerberg-
quietly-buries-the-metaverse

82   EqualOcean (2023) 'Will Apple's Vision Pro Save the Metaverse?',
Available at: https://equalocean.com/news/2023062519811

83   Politico (2022) 'Vestager: Metaverse poses new competition challenges',
Available at: https://www.politico.eu/article/metaverse-new-
competition-challenges-margrethe-vestager/

84   Pew Research Center (2022) 'The Metaverse in 2040', Available at:
https://www.pewresearch.org/internet/2022/06/30/the-metaverse-

in-2040/

85 McKinsey & Company (2022) 'Digital Twins: The Foundation of the Enterprise Metaverse', Available at: https://www.mckinsey.com/ capabilities/mckinsey-digital/our-insights/digital-twins-the-foundation-of-the-enterprise-metaverse

86 IAPP (2022) 'Metaverse and Privacy', Available at: https://iapp.org/news /a/metaverse-and-privacy-2/

CHAPTER SIX

87 Subramanian, S. *Quartz* 'Forty percent of all shipping cargo consists of fossil fuels'. January 14, 2022. https://qz.com/2113243/forty-percent-of-all-shipping-cargo-consists-of-fossil-fuels

88 European Parliament. (2015). 'Circular economy: definition, importance, and benefits'. Available at: https://www.europarl.europa.eu/news/en/ headlines/economy/20151201STO05603/circular-economy-definition-importance-and-benefits

89 Ellen MacArthur Foundation, Towards the circular economy Vol. 1: an economic and business rationale for an accelerated transition (2013).

90 Plastic Bank. (2022). 'Sustainability Report'. Available at: https://assets.plasticbank.com/wp-content/uploads/2023/06/ 16012405/Plastic-Bank-2022-Sustainability-Report-min.pdf

91 Cefic. (no date). 'Safe and Sustainable by Design'. Available at: https://cefic.org/a-solution-provider-for-sustainability/safe-and-sustainable-by-design/

92 Patrick Parsons. 'Sustainable by Design Report'. Jan 2022. https://www.patrickparsons.co.uk/wp-content/uploads/Sustainable-by-Design-Report-Web.pdf

93 International Renewable Energy Agency (IRENA). (2022). 'Renewable Energy Targets in NDCs' (p. 24). Available at: https://www.irena.org/-/media/Files/IRENA/Agency/Publication/ 2022/Jan/IRENA_NDCs_RE_Targets_2022.pdf

94 Jolly, J. 'AI helps airline pilots avoid areas that create polluting contrails'. The Guardian. 9 Aug 2023. https://www.theguardian. com/environment/2023/aug/09/ai-helps-airline-pilots-avoid-are as-that-create-polluting-contrails

CONCLUSION

95   Savage, R. 'What is a BRICS currency and is the U.S. dollar in trouble?' *Reuters*, 24 Aug 2023. https://www.reuters.com/markets/currencies/what-is-brics-currency-could-one-be-adopted-2023-08-23/

96   Akolkar, B. 'Bitcoin: Brazil and BRICS Countries to Create Global Currency to Boost Trillion-Dollar Business with China'. *Crypto News Flash*, 29 May 2023. https://www.crypto-news-flash.com/bitcoin-brazil-and-brics-countries-to-create-global-currency-to-boost-trillion-dollar-business-with-china/

97   https://thebulletin.org/doomsday-clock/current-time/

www.ingramcontent.com/pod-product-compliance
Lightning Source LLC
LaVergne TN
LVHW041209050326
832903LV00021B/550